# DO YOU HAVE A

## Best Friend

# AT WORK?

### How Friday Became the Day to Celebrate
### Your Best Friends at Work

# SAM QUEENO

Book Cover Design and Interior Formatting by 100Covers.
Edited by Kaitlin Brennan, Stan Partlow

ISBN: 979-8-9897585-0-0
Printed in the United States of America

# Contents

*"No! Try not. Do. Or do not. There is no try."*

– Yoda

# Foreword

I FIRST MET Sam Queeno in August of 2021. It was one of the most unique introductions I've had in my nearly 30-year career in HR. Sam walked into my office wearing a Winnie the Pooh costume and offered me a stick of honey. The levity of this meeting was my first glimpse of Sam's unique approach to creating cultural change. I quickly learned having a first meeting with Sam where he was in a costume wasn't unusual. It was a visual presentation of why he's a well-known leader at American Electric Power (AEP) who has shown what's possible when a positive person undertakes a cause.

During my career, I've had the opportunity to work at large industrial companies with employee populations that spanned the globe. Leading Human Resources functions on this scale have taught me that an organization's culture is much more than what's said by the CEO. Culture is built over time by the discussions, actions and relationships that happen across a company. This is what makes company culture so resilient and difficult to change.

Managing change is one of the most difficult tasks faced by leaders. Corporations spend billions of dollars a year on consultants and plans to help their organizations navigate change. Yet, one of the most powerful catalysts for transforming a company's culture is when individual employees and leaders take ownership for positively impacting their influence. This type of organic, decentralized ownership of culture is unusual, and it's what brought Sam to my door dressed as a bear.

Many large companies use the Gallup Employee Engagement Survey to measure employee engagement and satisfaction. For some companies, there's one question that can be controversial – I have a best friend at work.

This question was a non-starter when it debuted at AEP more than a decade ago. We're a company with an engineer-heavy mindset. Our employees took this question literally. If their best friend didn't work for the company, then they didn't have a best friend at work. They also didn't see the point of the question, but Sam did, and it's no surprise he has drawn best friends at work. He leads with positivity and empathy, and he balances humility and firmness.

A best friend at work doesn't have to be your best friend in the real world (if you're lucky, sometimes they make that jump). A BFAW, as Sam calls them, is someone you can trust. They have your back and are ready to lend an ear. Having this person can vastly improve an employee's experience at work.

Every organization depends on people to be successful. From the smallest family business to the largest global enterprises, commerce doesn't happen without people. Leaders are responsible for creating an environment where the team can be their best. Eventually every leader comes to a place where they realize that improving the culture is an important lever to improving the environment for the team and delivering better outcomes for the customers and shareholders.

While there is no substitute for having the right 'tone at the top', Sam Queeno has shown how powerful one individual can be when they take ownership over something about which they're passionate. While "Do You Have a Best Friend at Work" focuses on one leader's opportunity to positively impact an organization's culture by creating Best Friends at Work (BFAW), it is about one man, showing up every day and intentionally making a positive impact in every decision, every action and with every person he encounters. Whether he's getting *SLAP*ped or finding his WHY, Sam lays out a framework for others to find their passion and purpose at work and in life. I can only image the world we could create if we got *SLAP*ped a little more often!

Phillip R Ulrich
EVP Chief Human Resource Officer, American Electric Power

# CHAPTER 1

I FLY A lot for work. And when I do, I typically fly American Airlines. So now I also fly it any other time I can. At some point, I got sucked into the whole airline "status" program because I kept getting points on American. If I absolutely must fly on another airline, all I can think about is how many points I just lost out on. Yep, I have a slight issue when it comes to achieving that top tier, for reasons I just cannot explain.

9D is my seat. The second my flight booking goes through; I open my app and select 9D. If it is not available, I move back a row to 10D, or even worse, to the left side in 9C, but I know I will not have a good flight in that seat. On the other hand, occasionally my "status" will get me upgraded to first class, which leaves me feeling a tad special for the time while on the flight. When I do not get a coveted free upgrade, 9D is my happy place. However, it is still painful watching the higher status passengers with their better snacks and ceramic coffee cups looking so comfortable.

If you haven't closed the book by now, I'm sort of impressed, and appreciate you sticking with me. I started writing this book while on a flight from Dallas to Columbus (my normal route home, DFW-CMH). Sitting in 9D, with all my excitement and ideas in my head, I thought to myself "this time I can actually do it." During my time in 9D, I typically read leadership or self-help type books. I like a book that I can learn something from and immediately apply to my life. I don't often find myself reading for pure enjoyment or reading a lot of fiction. So based on the type of books I like to read, and the sheer amount of time I spend in 9D, I figure I am qualified to write one as well. At this point we will still have to see, I may stop writing when this flight lands in CBUS, and who knows if I'll pick it back up again. Although if you're reading this, I guess I've finished it.

Hopefully it is going to be worth it to you, and lucky for me, after you purchase a book there are no refunds even if you think the book sucked. I was talking recently with my Best Friend Stan (you're going to hear A LOT about my Yoda) about a mutual acquaintance who wrote a book. I said to Stan, "If he ever asked you what you thought about the book, would you really tell him, a person who you actually know, that the book was horrible and how in the world could he write that?" No, I don't think most rational people would say that, and neither did Stan.

People may politely say it was good or give minor feedback, but it's unlikely they would tell you to your face that it sucked. You see, I have been thinking about writing a book for several years, but have doubted anyone would want to read a book by Sam Queeno, and who am I to write a book or give advice? As you can probably tell by now, I have no idea how to actually write a book and I am guessing that writing it this way isn't the traditional way to do it, but this is the only way I know how, and the only way I want to — writing down my thoughts like I am talking to you as I sit here in 9D.

So, this is my attempt to do something that I have been wanting to do for a while. I really did not get serious about it until a few things in my life happened near simultaneously:

1.  Best Friend Friday (BFF) started gaining some popularity (for me, three people commenting on my post = popular)

2.  My best friend in life —my wife, Gina— out of the blue as we were talking about BFF, mentioned that I should write a book, and

3.  I had just finished reading the brilliant book *YOU, ME, WE Why We All Need a Friend at Work,* by authors Morag Barrett, Eric Spencer, and Ruby Vesely.

I finished reading Barrett, Spencer, and Vesely's book in 9D on a trip to Corpus Christi, TX (I got upgraded to first class on the way down, so I was in a great mood). Their book, in my opinion, lays out a path for everyone on how to become a best friend at work. While I was reading, I realized that this was the kind of thing I had wanted to do for so long with Best Friend Friday, but I didn't have a roadmap to explain the WHY behind what I was doing. If you somehow are not one of my three commenters and have not heard about BFF, you can find me and Best Friend Friday on LinkedIn.

**linkedin.com/in/sam-queeno-cpp®-8205b2100**
**linkedin.com/company/best-friend-friday**

Now that I had finished reading their book, I was motivated and I finally had a guide to tell my story — to explain this BFF thing I do every Friday and what it is I am trying to accomplish, and where we can all go from here.

So, what is this book about really? Leadership? Ha! It seems funny to me say out loud (or rather, in writing) that I am going to give you advice about leadership. I can probably write a few chapters on what NOT to do as a leader...I've got plenty of those stories. Or could this be about how, deep down I am afraid I suck as a leader, but I continue to work on my craft and play the infinite game (thank you Simon Sinek, my hero). So then, is this a book about building culture? Sure, we can go with that. Remember the Best Friend Friday thing you followed on LinkedIn during the last paragraph?

I actually started Best Friend Friday to appease my boss (aka Yoda, aka Best Friend Stan) so he would stop asking our team what we were doing about the "I have a best friend at work" question on Gallup's Q12® survey. At this point in my book journey with you, I still don't have a clue what I want it to be about. I know one thing; I don't want this to be a boring book. I want to have fun writing it and putting my thoughts down on paper. I am writing this as a test for myself to see if I can really do this. Then again, I'm still sitting in 9D on my way from DFW to CMH and writing this is keeping me entertained while on this flight, so there is a good chance this is just a pipe dream and I'll never pick it back up.

If I actually finish writing this book, I won't call it a "leadership" book because the truth is, I don't see myself as a great leader. I have many issues and flaws, and I don't think I am accomplished enough to give leadership advice. I have seen great leaders in action. I worked for one for 15 years —Stan Partlow, my Jedi Master, and we both worked for another —Nick Akins former CEO of American Electric Power. They are the type of leader I aspire to be. Okay at this point, I guess I do have to decide what I want this book to really be about. What will someone who picks this up expect to learn?

This book is not going to preach to you about what it takes to be a better leader. Over my many screw ups, I have learned one important lesson that has stuck with me. No matter what is presented to us or what we are dealing with in our lives, we all have a choice, and how you show up every day is a choice. I will tell you this, as a leader you have the power to change someone's life, to make something better, to make a difference. So, if what you are expecting in this book is a play by play that says, "do this, do that, use this tool for x," then this is not the book for you. Okay, that did sound a little preachy. I want to use this book to share my leadership journey and to talk about several people that have had an impact on me.

You may now be asking yourself why you would want to hear about Sam Queeno's leadership journey. I couldn't agree more, but I am the one writing this book and you are the one reading it, so we might as well talk about something. We will discuss Best Friend Friday and the Best Friend at Work (BFAW) model. However, this framework will not be what you've seen in other books, there is no step-by-step blueprint, there are no checklists. If we're being honest, how many of us have read a leadership book and then actually applied everything we've "learned" in it. If you have, I am impressed. There have been some books that I have read over and over again, and others where, like those Ron Popeil infomercials, the inventor who coined the phrase, I "set it and forget it." Which means as soon as I land in Columbus, I am done reading the book and I instantly forget it. I'm not saying the book was bad, it may have given me some nuggets to think about and a few things I could apply to my life, but overall, it just didn't stick in my memory.

I want this book to stick, and I want to take you along with me on my leadership journey — what I thought leadership was, and how I see it now in the present day. What I'm hoping and expecting to happen as you read on, is that my journey will resonate with you and that you'll chuckle a little along the way. You are going to get some of the leadership nuggets that I've picked up, or came up with myself, and some stories that have happened to me that may help you on your own journey. I guess I want this book to somewhat be about leadership, culture, best friends at work, and FUN.

Leadership is hard, I will be the first to admit that. Sometimes, it can feel like you're pushing a boulder up a hill, and then it slips, hits you, and you're at the bottom again, with a boulder on top of you. Now you must get up and start pushing up again. Why would anyone want to do this? Some may choose management because it pays more, and they want to make more money. If that is what is driving you to become a leader, you will be sorely mistaken. First of all, if you do this leadership thing right, you'll be working more than your employees, so what your paid for is not defined by 8 hours. Second, if money is what motivates you and your defining your success by how much of it you make, you are not going to succeed in leadership.

However, if you do happen to think that way and you picked up this book, you're in luck because I'm going to *SLAP* you into becoming a better you. I *SLAP* myself daily. This is my driving force and a leadership principle I think all leaders should live by. **S**erve, **L**ove, **A**ction, **P**assion is the HOW a leader should show up. But for that to work, as a leader, you need to find your WHY. I promise we will get into all of this, but it won't make any sense to you without introducing "Bad Sam," and explaining how I got to this place. I can assure you that in the past I never thought about this, or cared about culture and this touchy, feeling emotional stuff as a leader. As "Bad Sam," I thought it was my job as a manager to ensure that everyone who worked for me got their job done and that we all earned our money. I thought a leader was supposed to be a smarter, more competent worker than the people they led. I thought it wasn't my problem if my staff member had marriage issues or had trouble getting to work because I was paying them to do a job, so they had better get to work.

I realize what I have just described as the beginning of my leadership journey may resonate with some of you. Either you think the same way about leading people, or you know a person like Bad Sam. It is very common for people managers to think that getting involved in the personal lives of their staff or opening up to their employees about their personal life is inappropriate. Work and home are separate, and when it blends it creates problems. They believe that we do not come to work to make friends — this is a business, and we should act like it.

It sounds harsh, but when I first became a "leader," that is how I thought. I put "leader" in quotes because in the early stages of my career, I had no business calling myself a leader. I thought I was a leader because of my title and because I was paid slightly more than when I was an individual contributor, but I didn't know squat about what truly meant to be a leader. My understanding of leadership didn't come until years later, with the help of many people that knew better than I did and decided to help me. They never forced it on me, I had to be open to changing my ways and to getting better at my craft to become the type of leader that I aspired to be.

I am fortunate to have had mentors in my life that saw something in me that I couldn't see in myself, and who invested their time and energy in supporting me. If it wasn't for those true leaders, I wouldn't have lasted as a leader. Looking back now, I cringe at the thought of that guy (Bad Sam), but it's all I knew at the time, and I didn't think there was anything wrong with it. The work got done, I was a very hard worker. My team accomplished their tasks and we all got paid. What more did I need to do for them as their "leader"?

By writing this book, I want to be able to tell the story of Best Friend Friday, its true purpose, and how we as leaders can drive change. Anyone can be a leader. You don't need a special title (some people do have cool titles though) and guess what, you need to lead yourself before you can lead others (I picked that tidbit up somewhere). I want to write something that you can read with a little laughter, some nuggets of "wisdom," or more likely in my case, some advice on what not to do as a leader. I figure if I talk about my journey and how I got to this point (Me! Writing a book!), you may gain some knowledge of how to show up as a better leader.

I hope that I can share with you purpose behind BFF and how this movement can change the world! Yep, I said it, Chapter 1 needed a big bold statement like that to really get your attention. Did it work? Honestly, I do believe that having best friends at work can change the world. If everyone around the world spent time treating each other like they would treat a best friend, we could solve a lot of our issues.

I know there will be those of you that pick this up just because you are my friends (THANK YOU), and I know I am going to give some away so that I can say they are flying off the shelf. Obviously, I also want you to get something out of it — heck you did spend your hard-earned money on it (although it's entirely possible that I gave you a free copy). So, if this is the last page you are going to read, I want to thank you for making it this far, and want to leave you with a little nugget of wisdom before you go:

*"You have to go Left before you can go Right"* – Shelene Bryan

That nugget won't make sense to you, but you decided not to read further. For the others who have chosen to continue reading, you are now going Left.

Ultimately, this is the story of an Italian kid from Buffalo, New York, who fell into the security industry. In the remaining chapters of this book, I will explain my leadership journey and how certain events in my life led me to create Best Friend Friday. You will understand that BFF is a movement and the BFAW model just might change the world. So, I must ask…

Are you ready to get *SLAP*ped?!

# CHAPTER 2

# The Italian from Buffalo

IN ORDER FOR you to understand me now, we need to start at the beginning to help you see how I'm wired. I promise I'm not going to start on the day I entered this world, because no one wants to read that far back, and this book is not about me. It is about helping others, but first I'll give you an understanding of how I got to where I am today.

I loved growing up as an Italian American in Buffalo, NY. The Godfather movies really resonated with me, and I thought of myself as the tough guy Guido with gold chains, a pinky ring, and track suit. I was an altar boy and did everything that was expected of a young boy growing up in an Italian family. I learned early on from my parents that nothing is given, and you must work hard to accomplish anything. I started working at a very young age and held a job all throughout my teenage years. Work was always a priority, and it was engrained in me that you never left a job until you had another ready to start. You always gave two-week notice and never did anything to harm your family name.

Since work was such a big part of my upbringing, that was my number one priority. I know that sounds shitty, but I thought of it as my responsibility to make sure my family was taken care of, and that would be very hard to do without a job. So, it was job, family, everything else. I would like to say over time I figured out that was backwards even though I would do anything for my family, but there is still part of me that will always feel, if I'm not performing at the level I'm paid to do, my family could suffer. Luckily, I'm blessed to have an amazing Best Friend, my wife Gina, who understands how screwed up I am, but also understands the Italian culture since she is an Italian princess.

Gina and I met in the high school cafeteria during lunch. Our parents already knew each other, and her father told my mother that we were at the same school. When I heard that, I had to seek her out and after I finally figured out who she was, I decided to approach her and ask her out. I'm pretty sure I didn't ask her on a date the very first time we met, I had to be smoother than that, but you'll have to confirm that with her. Eventually I worked up the courage, and here we are now married with three amazing boys — Sammy, Vinny, and Joey.

Since Gina and I have been together pretty much since our teenage years, I like to refer to my childhood timeline as BG (Before Gina). In my BG years, starting around 10 or 11 years old, I had always wanted to be in the military. I joined the civil air patrol when I was 13 and the Junior Reserve Officers' Training Corps (JROTC) during high school. I eventually decided I wanted to join the Army and become a tank commander. Because I am not vertically gifted (aka short), I was told tanks were the way to go.

My junior year of high school, I became more serious and began applying to several military schools with ROTC programs. I was accepted into the Citadel and Norwich University. I knew I would need to work on my physical training, but these schools would help me do that. I have always had issues passing the timed running for physical fitness (PT) tests. I'm the fat Italian kid that used to be skinny, but I think one day all the pasta caught up with me. I have always battled with my weight, but I also hate exercise. I knew I'd never do it on my own, but if I was forced to do daily PT I could get there.

I decided to attend Norwich University, and after my four years there I would get a commission into the Army. I felt a calling to service and serving others, and I thought the way to meet my calling was in the military. There is no greater honor than serving your country and helping others. Unfortunately, I also thought that in order to do this, I had to fully commit myself and have no attachments. I decided to go and break up with Gina, so I didn't have anything tying me down. Now in my senior year, I had no girlfriend and just needed to get through graduation and go off to college.

I am a true believer that we don't control our destinies and that God has mapped out everything for us already. There may be times in your life that you go off one path and down another, but you'll end up in the place you were really meant to be. I had my plan all mapped out, but there was just one little flaw with my plan — I was still in love with Gina, so even though we were broken up, we did what all teenagers do, and still saw each other from time to time.

Two months after I graduated from high school, I was on my way to Vermont to report to Norwich University. My mom and dad drove me to school with a couple of extra passengers. Gina and our one-month-old son, Sammy, came with us to see me off. Yep, you read that right, we were teenage parents. Ten months earlier, I found out I was going to be a father. I can tell you the first thing that popped into my mind was "your life is over," and the second thought was probably "what are your parents going to say?" After that it was like being on a roller coaster, and it was not a fun rollercoaster. There were many tears, joy, and worry from everyone involved.

Now I am not going to describe to you the entire nine months and what transpired because it is highly personal and private, but if you have seen the movies or shows and have heard the statistics about "babies having babies" (I always thought that saying was funny) then you can imagine what it was like. I am telling you this because I didn't know this at the time, but this event in my life was the best thing that ever could have happened to me. Yes, I was a scared teenager and had no idea what was going to happen, but there was one thing I knew for sure, I now had two lives to take care of for the rest of my life.

I always knew I would get married and have a family, I just didn't know when. So, my plan was simple, I would go to school, get my commission through ROTC, and then marry Gina and we would be together forever. See, Gina was supportive of me going to school — she knew it was my dream and didn't want me to resent her or Sammy. I knew being away Gina would be alright, she is an amazing mother and always wanted to be a mom. She had both my family and hers to support her in whatever she needed.

In Italian culture, the first grandson is a big deal, with Sammy's birth we had kept the family name alive for another generation, so Gina would have help with anything she needed. Not that she asked for much help or needed it, she was all in as a fulltime mom and did everything she and Sammy needed.

It was hard for me to leave them and go off to school, but I told myself that this was the only way I could truly take care of my family. I didn't see any other options in front of me. The one thing I did know was that I was not going to be a statistic, meaning I was not going to be "that guy" who gets his girlfriend pregnant and then leaves.

I went to school before cell phones were popular or affordable and being at a military school meant that you couldn't just call anytime you wanted. You basically are shut off from the outside world and essentially have no rights. In our first semester, my classmates and I were not "recognized" as cadets yet. When we were allowed to call, it was only for five minutes, which is not enough time to really connect. Letter writing was the only real form of communication during that first semester. I wrote Gina letters daily.

As the semester ended and I was close to becoming a recognized cadet, I had an awakening — I couldn't do this for another three and half years. I felt I was neglecting my responsibilities and needed to be with Gina and Sammy. I made the difficult decision to leave school. No one pressured me and a lot of people were shocked when I finally made that hard decision. I believe that being in the military brings you honor and that the men and women in uniform are heroes, and I was ashamed of myself for quitting, but the little voice inside of me that I kept hearing was "family."

I left school in November and married Gina the following January. The Norwich eagle I used to wear on my hat is now tattooed on me with the words, Family and Honor. I figured out that you don't need to wear a patch on your uniform to have honor. It is you as a person and your actions that define you. From that day on, I was determined not to fail myself or my family, and that I would be successful.

One of the first jobs I took to when I came back from school was being a Security Guard. Originally, I was drawn to that profession because I thought being a bouncer was cool. Even though I never ended up working as a bouncer, I have held various jobs in the security profession, either as a primary or a secondary job. I have had to work second jobs throughout most of my marriage to make ends meet. I have been a donut maker, a produce clerk, I've cleaned movie theaters, been a night shift desk clerk at a motel, and have

been an Emergency Medical Technician. I did all this all while trying to go to school closer to home, which I did a miserably bad job
at and while continuing to add to our debt. I knew my parents were
upset that I left Norwich, and even though they never would have
said it, I felt I had to prove that I could still do what I needed to do
and also be home with my family.

I wasn't successful at balancing two full time jobs and school,
so I ended up leaving school for a second time and not finishing
college until late in my career. The one constant throughout my
time in Buffalo was that I always enjoyed my security work. Maybe
it was the uniform, or the mission of protecting people and prop-
erty. I know some people look down on the security profession as a
whole and yes it does have its challenges, but I never did. There are
more private security officers in this country than there are police
officers. Even though their missions are different, they are still part
of the first responder community. There are so many different types
of positions within the security profession, and the men and women
that I have come to know during my career are some of the most
passionate and amazing best friends I know.

My first taste of being a leader, and I use that term lightly at
this point in my journey, was as the second shift supervisor of security officers at a manufacturing plant in Buffalo. I was a boss, or
someone who thought being the boss meant you were in charge of
other people and was in no way a real leader. My role was to ensure
that the work got done and people who I was in charge of got to
work and got their work done. I led a team of 3 people who worked
from 3pm until 11pm. We reported to a site supervisor who oversaw
the entire security force.

Back then I was driven to do the best I could and ensure that
my team was the best they could be so that I could move up and
get promoted to the next level. I was never really given any roadmap on how to be a leader, and just like in most companies, the

hardest worker is usually the one that gets promoted. That doesn't necessarily mean that person will make a good leader, it just means that they may perform better than others in the department, and the next place for them is a promotion to leadership.

I sucked as a leader…I sucked really bad. I was never formally shown how to do the job and didn't have anyone to guide me early on. I thought my role was simply to produce results and if the people that I was charged to lead were not producing like I was, then a change was needed. It was not about coaching, guiding, or having one-on-one meetings with team members. It was more like, "Hey Jim you're late again, I am writing you up," or, "Ron, you're missing your patrol rounds. I guess I need to watch and see what you're doing wrong." I felt that my job revolved around correcting my team all the time.

I would love to say that I wasn't like this for very long and that I figured out pretty quickly that it was not the right way to lead, but that would be a lie. As I got promoted in the security profession and took on other management roles, I changed a little. I say a little because maybe I softened a bit, but I still felt that I had to drive the team to success. It was all about getting the job done and honestly, I never thought about the people. We were being paid to do a job and perform, and if you were not performing it was your problem and you needed to fix it.

There are a lot of YOU's in there, right? YOU, YOU, YOU! The WE never crossed my mind for a second. It took many years and many great leaders in my life to change how I lead. I think that leaders and mentors are the most important element in anyone's professional journey. You take your queues from the person that leads you. I was blessed to finally connect with true leaders that helped guide me to "see the light." That, and a combination of self-reflection, learning, and leadership programs benefitted me greatly. Over time, my leadership style did change, and it changed for the better, but there was still room to grow.

Even today as I am writing this book, I am working on being a better leader. You're never done learning; you must become a lifelong learner in anything you do. I have chosen leadership as my craft and I want to continually be better at my craft, so I must keep learning and adapting. It took a long time, but eventually I realized that leadership was about People first and not the work. Once I figured that part out, the work part was easier. Not perfect, because leadership is HARD. During an event, I once met Shelene Bryan, a former Hollywood producer and founder of skip1.org, who said "you have to go Left to go Right." She made this statement during a pre-event meet and greet and was talking about leadership and doing something that matters. Left stood for:

Love

Effort

Focus

Toughness

These were qualities she felt were needed in a leader. If you want to be the "Right" leader, you must start by going Left. In her keynote later that morning, she made another statement that I have not forgotten to this day. It is one of the reasons I wake up every morning and live my WHY. She stated, "I'm not worried you are going to fail at anything, my fear is you might succeed at something that doesn't matter." From that day on I wanted to make sure what I was doing mattered. What that was exactly, was yet to be determined.

# CHAPTER 3

# Sometimes you just need to get SLAPped (a lot)

LUCKY FOR ME, I had people in my life that slapped some sense into me whenever I needed it. I have become a better human because of being slapped. Now, I'm not talking about the actual physical act of slapping, but sometimes in life we all want to slap something! I am referring to the **Serve, Love, Action, Passion** driving force, which I try to live by.

I did not come up with this alone. I volunteered as a board member for a former non-profit in Columbus, Ohio that I was very passionate about. It was a leadership development organization, and during one of our board annual retreats we came up with this as our purpose, sort of our "mission statement." The words really resonated with me, probably because I'm an acronym junkie, so I loved to say, "we are going to *SLAP* the leadership in you!" Okay, so that catch phrase didn't stick for any marketing purposes, but the individual words had real meaning and propelled me to think about how I show up every day.

## Serve

This stems from servant leadership, which I realize is hard for some people to swallow. Those people are the "poor" leaders in my opinion. If you are a leader or want to become a leader, guess what folks, you are serving others. The people under your charge are your purpose as a leader — you should be working for them. There are many definitions of servant leadership, and I cannot count the number of books I have read on the subject, so I am not going to waste your time by talking about the servant leadership principles. What I am going to do is explain how "Serve" is a driving force.

If you are in serve mode, you are looking for the win-win in situations, and you are more willing to put others before yourself. You are looking for the compromises in situations and you know what to do with that ego of yours? You must put that in your back pocket. Serving is hard, there is no doubt about that.

I never used to have the Serve mentality early on in my leadership journey. Remember — I am the guy that only cared about getting the work done. But if you have a Serve mindsight, I think your heart opens just a little bit more because you want to do right by others. You fundamentally are thinking about others first and how your actions affect others. In my opinion, Serve is not just a leadership principle, it is a human principle. If you think about it for a minute, there are things you do in your daily life that might fall under the serve principle. Giving someone a ride, paying it forward to someone in the drive thru behind you, or offering help to someone who might be struggling or needs someone to talk to. You are serving a fellow human in one way or the other.

If you wake up every day and say to yourself, "I am going to brighten someone's day today by calling them and telling them how much they mean to me," you're serving them, because you're making them feel good. That is my driving force. I try every day to serve everyone, including myself. If I am not serving myself first, I am not able to be my best for everyone else. Now, is it all rainbows and unicorns?? NO. I suck sometimes, as we all do. Heck, I have bad days, but I strive to serve daily in one way or another. It could be little things that you do, and you may not even realize that you are serving but trying to put yourself in that frame of mind will allow you to make this world better.

What I have found is that serving others makes you feel much better. Do you remember the saying "it is better to give than receive?" For the longest time, I thought that was stupid. I want a gift! But when I began giving more in my life it truly made me much happier than receiving something. I think a lot of it has to do with the other person — how it makes them feel to receive the gift will resonate with you and that is the gift that you get in return.

Now, I mentioned earlier that you have to serve yourself first before you can truly serve others. The saying "you have to put your oxygen mask on first before you put on others" makes sense to me. You cannot truly serve anyone if you are not first serving yourself.

### Love

Oh boy here we go, the L word… Now right off the bat people start thinking you can't say that at work. You cannot tell your employee you love them. Well, I am not talking about Love, like how you love your spouse or partner, that's physical love. I am talking about Loving them like they mean something to you. Loving them in the sense that you care deeply about their lives and the lives of their families. Hurting when they hurt, just being a person, they can come to no matter if it is work or personal. You Love them so much that you may need to have that hard conversation about poor performance.

The word Love is hard for people, especially in a work environment. Heck, it was hard for me. I am the Security guy, and I am supposed to "Love" people? I thought I needed to be the "hard ass." This very concept was probably the hardest for me to figure out and accept. When I finally did, my eyes opened, and I started to become a better person.

Love has taught me humility, vulnerability, empathy, and kindness. Traits we should all practice but are even more important for individuals in leadership roles to embody.

Love is complicated, but it doesn't need to be. I genuinely Love people, and I would do anything for anyone if they asked and it was within my control. I care about people, especially their Safety. My Why in life is "Striving to Make the World a Safer Place to Live, Work, and Play" ® We will dissect my trademark WHY later in another chapter but for now, I couldn't have figured that out if I wasn't in a place of Love.

I get it that not many people in leadership positions think of loving the people they are supposed to serve — their employees. I was one of them; I never felt that it was appropriate to get involved in my employees' lives. They were there to do a job and I was managing them to complete that job. I was dead wrong, and it took me many years and many mentors and training courses to figure out that Love is something every leader must focus on.

As a leader, you technically hold your employees' livelihood in your hands. If you think about it, you may be the one that decides how much of a raise someone gets, if someone can go on vacation or not, how much their annual bonus is, and if they receive a promotion. Also, let's say you're really an asshole at work and your employees hate working for you because you're making them miserable. Do you think that could bleed over into their personal lives? Of course, it could.

Hating the person, you work for is a horrible position to be in. I have found that if you lead with Love, even if you must let someone go for poor performance, you probably have done everything you could over a period of time to try and not get to that point. However, if it has come to that, you are not doing that person any good by letting them stay and continue down this path. If you are leading with Love, you will know you have done everything you could because you Love that person. Love is a powerful thing and if you are not leading with Love you're not leading.

## Action

Action should be one of the simplest things to understand, but many of us fail at it. If you want to get something done or to achieve something you must take Action. Simple right? But so many people do not take action and expect that "it" will magically happen, or their problems will solve themselves. Now I don't want you to confuse Action with accomplishing something. That is usually the byproduct of the Action; in my mind, Action literally means in doing something. Regardless of whether you know the outcome, and even if you have no idea how to do something, if it is something you want to do, then do it! That's Action!

I am a huge Star Wars fan and try to tie many things in my life back to the Star Wars movies. If you have seen any Star Wars movies it boils down to good vs. evil. However, what I love about it the most is it is a bunch of Best Friends, the Rebels who took action to defeat the evil galactic empire. My two favorite characters are R2D2 and Yoda. I am telling you this because I live by Jedi Master Yoda quotes, and one of his most recognizable is "Do or Do Not, there is no Try". The DO in that quote is all about Action. If there is something you want to do, take the action needed and get it done. Even if you fail at it, you took the action to start and hopefully you learned something from that failure, so continue with your action.

I find so many times in life, both personally and professionally, that we talk way too much. Sometimes you need to have a conversation to understand what may need to happen or how to start, I get that, but what I am talking about is the constant conversations, or the meetings where continual roadblocks go up, or the negative people that use that C word I hate. Do you know that word, that word that kills action? I don't even like writing it down because when I hear it, I always want to say, "why not?" And this word started off so good at first, but someone went ahead and threw an apostrophe "t" at the end and screwed it up. So, let's agree that in order for Action to work you must tell yourself it CAN happen, and we will all make a point to never use the apostrophe "t" and just leave CAN alone.

I think many people don't take action not because they are afraid, but because they just don't know or are unable to see the end result, so they don't start something. When I created Best Friend Friday, I had no idea what the end game was or how it would be received. I just took Action and did something. We will get into Best Friend Friday in our next chapter, but I bring this up because sometimes you don't have all the answers yet, or don't even know how to start, but committing to taking action is the start, and now you just need to figure out the rest of the journey.

In the context I have been discussing, Action is not some grand gesture or a call to action to achieve all your life goals. It is a literally concept to live by and it can be as simple is taking action to apologize and say you're sorry to someone. Or taking the action to admit you were wrong to your employees.

Taking action is doing something, which could, and I know this might be confusing, include not doing something. You read that right, there are times that not doing something is the action you need to take, but at least you are recognizing this and taking action.

For me, Action is getting shit done! I am impatient by nature and driven to get one thing done and then move on to the next. I like results and seeing accomplishments, made either by me or the team I serve. What I love about action is the doing part, getting into it and executing. Succeeding, failing, creating, these are all things I enjoy. Well not the failure part, I don't think anyone necessarily likes to fail, but I am of the mindset that you learn from failure, so even though the outcome sucks it is still great to learn something.

In order to succeed in anything in life, you have to have the mindset of Action. Don't wait to be told to do something do it if it needs to be done. Stop talking about what you want to do, or should do, and take action.

## Passion

Have you ever done anything in your life that you hated to do? There are some things that you can choose not to do. For example, if you don't like cutting the grass, you can hire a lawn service to cut it for you. With that in mind however, I am sure there are tasks or jobs in your life that you still must do but they are the last thing in the world you want to be doing. Maybe it is dealing with the budget at work. You might hate math and hate reviewing expenses, but know it is part of your management duties to review and report each month to your management. It is a task you hate doing but understand that it must be done. It is probably safe to say that you don't jump out of bed on that day and say "YES! The monthly numbers are out today, I cannot wait to dive into the monthly expenses!"

I am going to go out on a limb here, and if this is you when it comes to the budget, you have little to no passion. Passion drives results, plain in simple! If you are passionate about something, most likely you are going to give it your all to accomplish something. That is why Passion is an important factor in what we choose to take on. The more passion you have around a topic or a cause, the more effort you are going to put into it. If you hate your job, or hate being a leader, my first piece of advice to you is to find another job and that maybe leadership is not for you.

I know people have said if you're looking for a career, find something you are passionate about and do that, and you will never work a day in your life. Is that true? If you find that career you are passionate about, can you honestly say that it is not work because you are passionate about doing it? I think only you can answer that question, but I can tell you from my personal experience, the answer is yes for me (somedays). What I am saying is I am passionate about what I do, and love what I do, and yes, it is work, but I truly enjoy doing it. There are days I hate it, but there are more good days than there are bad, and I wake up excited to start my day.

Passion is not just about what you do for a living. It can be anything you decide to take on or accomplish. It may not be a true passion of yours, but it could be to someone on your team, or to your manager. For example, your manager may tell you that the leadership team wants us to really focus on making our organization culture the #1 in the company. You, as someone who Loves your boss and would do anything for him, are not passionate about culture. You think the whole culture thing at companies has been overplayed and it is just a buzzword companies use.

Your boss is passionate about this, and it shows when he is talking about it. So, because you have a great relationship with your boss, and you highly respect him and would do anything for him because he leads with Love, you put forth the effort because he is passionate about it, and you are passionate about your boss and don't want to let him down.

Passion is the fuel that keeps us going. A lack of passion can stall us out. Your passion for something can also be infectious to others. Think about speaking in front of a group of people regarding something you are passionate about. Naturally if you are truly passionate about it, it will be seen in your expressions, heard in your tone, and how you make them feel. Your passion will naturally come out if you truly believe in something. The people in the audience will respond based on your passion. I am sure you have experienced both sides of this, listening to someone who could care less what they were up there saying, and someone who was so passionate about something you wanted to jump right in with them. Passionate people draw in others to whatever they are trying to accomplish or say. The passion that people radiate can really have an effect on those around them and may cause them to look for their own passion. Be that driving force by having Passion.

Okay, by now I hope you have a little understanding of being *SLAPped*. You're probably wondering, what you can do to practice, or what specific actions you can take to *SLAP* yourself. As I explained to you in the first chapter, I have no idea how to write a book, so why would you think I would give you a guide to follow or a checklist?

*SLAP* is not something I can teach you or something you can learn by doing steps 1-5. *SLAP* is a state of mind. It's how you show up. It is a set of guiding principles that, over time, I hope will lead you to becoming a better leader and human. Serve, Love, Action, and Passion are principles you must embrace. I cannot teach you to Serve, I cannot teach you to Love, and it's up to you if you want to take Action. As for Passion, I cannot force you to be passionate about something. These are not concepts that come with a manual you can read on each topic (otherwise I would have provided it). You must choose to show up this way.

Now, there are books on these topics for sure, and likely far better than what I am writing. I have read probably a dozen leadership books on servant leadership. And yes, I learned something about servant leadership from them, but ultimately it was up to me to decide if I was going to be a servant leader or not. *SLAP,* in its simplest form, is a choice you make today. Are you going to *SLAP* yourself and live these every day and strive to make this world better? I hope you do. So now you can say you got *SLAPped* by Sam (just keep my last name out of it).

# CHAPTER 4

# I Have a Best Friend at Work

SERIOUSLY GALLUP, WHY in the world would you put that question on your Q12® Employee Engagement Survey. I have a best friend at work? That was the question I first asked when the company I work for —American Electric Power (AEP)— engaged Gallup as part of a company-wide culture journey. If you're not familiar with Gallup's engagement survey, you can check it out at **www. gallup.com**. I encourage you to check it out and read the science behind their questions. As I'm writing, this is what is currently posted on their website:

## How to Measure Employee Engagement with the Q12

There are 12 needs managers can meet to improve employees' productivity. This approach to engagement is simple, and it works. These are the 12 employee needs that make up the items on Gallup's engagement survey:

1. I know what is expected of me at work.
2. I have the materials and equipment I need to do my work right.
3. At work, I have the opportunity to do what I do best every day.
4. In the last seven days, I have received recognition or praise for doing good work.
5. My supervisor, or someone at work, seems to care about me as a person.
6. There is someone at work who encourages my development.
7. At work, my opinions seem to count.
8. The mission or purpose of my company makes me feel my job is important.
9. My associates or fellow employees are committed to doing quality work.
10. **I have a best friend at work.**
11. In the last six months, someone at work has talked to me about my progress.
12. This last year, I have had opportunities at work to learn and grow.

According to Gallup's website, more than any other Q12 statement, "I have a best friend at work" tends to generate questions and skepticism. But there is one stubborn fact: It predicts performance.

I will be the first to tell you — they are not lying. Most people think this is an absolutely ridiculous statement and that it has no place at work. You do not come to work to make friends, and most people only have one best friend in their lifetime. Many people consider their spouse/partner/significant other as their best friend. As a leader, there is no way I can "force" my employees to be friends with each other. I could keep going on, telling you many of the comments I heard about that one statement after this survey was first introduced at AEP. A few of them were even made by me.

Initially, I didn't understand the importance of having best friends at work. Now don't get me wrong, I got along with a lot of my coworkers and enjoyed their company both at work and for an outside engagement from time to time. I, like many others in the company, mainly got hung up on the word "best" in that statement. I recall thinking to myself, "if the question asked do you have a friend at work, I probably could have given that a 5." Gallup's rating scale is 1-5, with 1 being a frustrated "no" and 5 being a strong "yes' but not necessarily perfection. The scale is a measure of subjective perceptions.

As a leader, my initial instinct was to look over the questions and think about which ones would be no brainers and easy to fix if the scores came in low. I did this before even seeing the results. Since the survey was open to all employees, I had to take it in addition to my employees, so as I answered the questions for myself, I also wrote down a list of smart-ass comments for how I would tackle each when the results came out.

1. I know what is expected of me at work.
   *Easy- give everyone their job descriptions so they know what is expected of them.*

2. I have the materials and equipment I need to do my work right.
   *Medium – Find out what everyone needs and if we can buy it, we will. If not tell them why. It shouldn't be that hard to do.*

3. At work, I have the opportunity to do what I do best every day.
   *Hard – I give them all opportunities, so let's hope that question gets high marks.*

4. In the last seven days, I have received recognition or praise for doing good work.
   *Easy – I'm pretty sure I thank my team and tell them they've done a good job, but I will make a better effort every 7 days.*

5. My supervisor, or someone at work, seems to care about me as a person.
   *Oh, I care about people… This one should be easy; I should just tell them I care.*

6. There is someone at work who encourages my development.
   *Easy, talk to people about their development opportunities.*

7. At work, my opinions seem to count.
   *Got this one covered, just do an opinion survey…*

8. The mission or purpose of my company makes me feel my job is important.
   *We have both our company-wide mission statement and our own mission statement in Security, so it shouldn't be that hard to tie it to their individual jobs.*

9. My associates or fellow employees are committed to doing quality work.
*No idea how to make them committed, but I think we are going to be okay here.*

10. **I have a best friend at work.**
*This one is going to be horrible, and there is no way we can make people become friends. Let's hope we don't have to do anything on this one.*

11. In the last six months, someone at work has talked to me about my progress.
*Easy - We just did mid-cycle performance reviews with everyone a few months ago, they should remember that.*

12. This last year, I have had opportunities at work to learn and grow.
*?????*

As I wrote down these questions, right off the bat I figured I would have to do some work when the results came out. With these types of work surveys, I think many people get overwhelmed and a little nervous, because if you are a team or group leader, you may equate these surveys as YOU (the leader) being rated. I had that initial thought, but after I took the survey, I really put it out of my mind until the results can back in.

I was not opposed to the company trying to transform our culture. Not that I had a vote in the initial effort anyway, but it just didn't really interest me back then. I had too many other priorities and I viewed myself as "the security guy," and was not into this "warm and fuzzy" stuff. Lucky for me, my mentor Stan Partlow (remember him from Chapter 1?) is just like Master Yoda and is a very wise leader. He understood the "why" and embraced the cultural transformation, ensuring that his team would as well. He is the kind of leader I aspire to become but can only keep striving to achieve.

If you want to learn directly from Stan you can go pick up his book on Amazon, *Leading Relentlessly*. You won't regret it and it will make you a better leader.

As Stan used his Jedi mind tricks on me, I started to embrace this "culture thing" as I was developing over time as a leader. I had gone through some leadership training, mentoring sessions, and had just begun to transform into a better leader. I still had setbacks sometimes (screw ups actually), but "setback" sounds better. Stan is good, but even he wasn't going to fix a screwed-up guy like me overnight. He likes to say that developing me into a leader was like water over a rock. He kept flowing over me and finally the rough rock (ME) was worn down to a smooth rock.

The one thing you need to understand about Stan is he is relentless, and when he has something on his mind, he doesn't let it go. He will drive you to achieve what he believes you can achieve, and he is the type of leader you want to please and perform for. He makes it hard to say no, and I cannot recall in the fourteen years I worked for him if I ever said no to him. Stan made us understand "why" culture was important and how this would benefit not only us personally, but our departments and the overall Security organization as well. Stan had the vision early on (Yoda stuff) that we could use culture to improve and advance our security program at the company. He also knew the company was changing, and as the saying goes, if you're not changing your dying. He knew it was time to embrace the culture and make the changes needed for the future.

It felt like the Christmas morning excitement of opening presents once the day had finally come. It was survey results day! Okay maybe the Christmas morning analogy is a little over the top because I wasn't excited at all. Once I remembered my password to log into the survey tool, I was met with a report that had two tabs, one for my direct reports and one for that showed everyone in my organization that reported up to me. The report kind of did look like

Christmas – it was full of green and red, showing how you compared to others in the company. After getting over the initial numbers, I started digesting what it all meant which questions I "did good on" and which ones "I sucked at". It doesn't quite say it in those terms, but that is how I felt at the time.

I cannot remember my scores exactly, but there were two that I knew were areas for improvement within my department – numbers 5 and 10. I assumed #10 was the best friend question, but #5 *"My supervisor, or someone at work, seems to care about me as a person,"* took me by surprise. I was blown away that members of my team thought I didn't care about them. I took it personally and knew I had to fix that somehow. The survey is not pass/fail, but I can tell you that from my point of view it's only natural to want to work on the areas that the survey highlights for improvement. So, we will get to #5 in a bit, but for now let's now focus on question 10 – having a best friend at work.

It was not just my team, other leaders and departments had the Best Friend at work question as an area for improvement as well. After the first year of results, the idea of "best friends at work" came up a lot as we talked about culture and culture plans. I sat in meeting after meeting where this topic was brought up, and people bashed it and were shocked that this question was there. Some suggested it be removed for the next survey. Over and over, I heard "excuses" for why we don't have best friends at work and how stupid the question was. These comments were not just coming from our Security organization, let me tell you; it was widespread. I heard it from other departments and coworkers I knew, and I even asked people outside of AEP what they thought. Mostly, people gave the same answer – that they don't have best friends at work.

Even today when I talk about our culture journey at various events and engagements, the first question I ask everyone in the audience is to raise their hands if they have best friends at work. I have never had 100% of the audience raise their hand. Now, Gallup doesn't just give you the survey and say have a nice day. They have the tools and improvement guides, and other good content for leaders to use as they work on each question. What they don't give you is a pass on that best friend question, it always stays in the survey.

Gallup encourages you as a department or organization, you to come up with a "culture action plan." This is a plan of what areas you want to improve on and how you are going to do that. You can pick any of the 12 questions, or other areas, it is your culture plan after all. AEP required every leader that received survey results to put together their culture plan collaboratively, working with their team members. So, for us at the Security Organization level, Stan had to have a plan for his entire organization, and then as one of his team leaders, I had to have a culture plan on what I wanted to accomplish for my department, and then individual managers had to have their own plans for their teams. Yes, that is a lot of plans, but they were important for our success.

As we looked at the Security Organization as whole, best friend at work was one of the areas for improvement, however neither we nor any other organization at that time was dumb enough to add that question to their plan, as far as I know. We didn't officially put best friend at work in the culture plan, which Stan was okay with (Jedi mind tricks ensued). He allowed his leaders to choose other topics to put in the plan, but he would continue to ask, "what are we doing about the best friend at work question?" He continually brought it up in staff meetings, in passing, or anytime culture was on an agenda for discussion. Remember when I said he was relentless? Well, he doesn't let things go.

So, I thought to myself, "I will do something about it," and I literally assigned everyone in my department a best friend. No, I am NOT kidding you here, I literally assigned each team member a best friend and said, "Summer, Rachel" you two are best friends. Meet regularly and get to know each other." Now, I was half joking, okay I was being a smart ass, but I thought it may succeed in getting everyone to answer that question better next time. When the survey came out again next year, I figured they would have to answer 4 or 5 right? Especially since I assigned them a best friend. Most people in the organization got a kick out of it, and even Stan would joke about it and tell people when the topic came up, "Sam assigned everyone a best friend." Stan doesn't do or say things like that by accident. I believe it was a Master Jedi mind trick to keep the topic of best friend at work going. It was maybe also his way of motivating me more on this topic.

*One-year passes…*

Year 2 survey results are in! The Security Organization's scores went up overall, but not on question #10. So, it's safe to say assigning best friends was not going to cut it. We regrouped as a leadership team, and I was hoping we would just celebrate that our scores went up overall and maybe, just maybe, Stan wouldn't bring up best friend at work. That thought lasted about thirty seconds. As I recall, it went something like this, "*Team we went up overall and that is because of everyone's effort this past year. Now we can't take our foot off the gas, and we need to keep driving to get even better. So, what are we doing about best friends at work?*" Are you effing kidding me! That was my inner voice speaking. I was literally saying to myself "let this shit go! It's a dumb ass question!" Well, we didn't let it go, as you may remember, I work for a guy who is relentless, so now what do we do?!

As time went on, I racked my brain trying to come up with what we could do about this. It was brought up in meetings, and I cannot recall all the ideas and discussion we had on this topic, but we discussed culture week after week. I am sure we tried a few things here and there, and we definitely made an effort to tackle this question and our culture as a whole. Then our two newest members joined the team — Babo and Wage. I have a minor obsession with online shopping, and Amazon makes things so easy. So, one day as I was looking for who knows what, I typed in the search bar "best friend toys." I quickly realized some…inappropriate results came up for that one, so I think I tweaked it and wrote stuffed toys or something like that.

Now you may ask yourself why I was searching for toys. Well, if you were to visit my conference room at work, it is filled with little toys, games, and candy. Meetings should be fun, so I like a conference room table filled with things we used to do as a child like Mr. Potato head, Simon, Rubik's cubes, Etch A Sketch, and a few small handheld video games. As I scrolled through the pages of results on Amazon, I found the Ugly Dolls and our soon to be best friends Babo and Wage.

If you are not familiar with Ugly Dolls, they actually turned them into an animated film in 2019, you can watch it here **http://www.uglydolls.com/**. However, the actual plush toys were created in 2001. Two of the characters, Babo and Wage, which were being sold together are actually best friends. They have a backstory for each of them that came with the plush toy, and it talks about them being best friends to each other. As I read more of the description, a light bulb went off. I think I said to myself "I've got the answer, I will BUY everyone a best friend!" Now let's be honest, buying a best friend is a little better than assigning best friends because who doesn't want a stuffed animal? I couldn't buy one for everyone in our organization, so I wasn't actually sure at that moment what I was going to do with my newly found assistants, but I bought several of them and tried to figure out what to do with them.

So as our new best friends arrived, I started giving them to people in a meeting or when I saw them in the hall, saying, "here is your best friend at work." My hope was that they would put them up in their cubicles or offices and talk about them, which would keep the best friend topic on peoples' minds. I continued to purchase more and more and then I recalled something I did when I was younger — Flat Stanley. In case you have no idea what I am taking about, Flat Stanley is a cut-out figure of this guy called Stanley that you were supposed to take all around with you, taking photos of him at different places, in different poses etc. Even parents would get in on this, taking their child's Flat Stanley to a work meeting out of town and snap a photo in front of a building or whatever. Once you collected photos of Flat Stanley, you were supposed to put a collage together and present it at school. It was a fun assignment, and I remember doing with my kids. So, I was thinking, what if we did a version of flat Stanley with Babo and Wage?

A lot of our culture initiatives that included Babo and Wage just happened by word of mouth. As we started giving Babo and Wage away to people, we told them to take pictures of themselves with their new best friends anywhere, including work, vacation, days off with family, literally anywhere. Then we asked them to send in their photos so we could showcase them each week. After snapping their photos, they were supposed to pass the dolls on to someone else in our department so another person could spend time with their new best friend at work. Our team rose to the challenge, and we were having a lot of fun with the new assignment.

Everyone was sending in pictures with the dolls in some really great places, doing different activities with their best friend. We spent that whole summer and into the fall taking pictures of Babo and Wage with our employees and other people in the company. We took these dolls everywhere, heck they were our best friends, and soon they became our unofficial mascot. At the peak of the fun, I think I had purchased 20+ dolls so that we had enough to go around.

To this day, I know of four that are left. I have no idea what happened to the rest of them. I think people just kept them after we stopped collecting photos, which I think is cool, because it shows that people got what we were trying to do and really enjoyed it.

*Some pictures of Babo and Wage with our employees on our culture board*

*Another year passes...*

Survey says, we went up! During the Babo and Wage fun, another survey came out for that year to gauge our engagement. I was happy to see that the score for Best Friend at work went up slightly, but it was still low compared to the other areas. I was happy with the improvement and figured we had tried everything we could, so it was not because of a lack of effort. I thought we just needed to realize we were chasing a unicorn here and that we should be happy with the results.

That is exactly what Stan told us, he was happy with the results, BUT "what are we doing about Best Friends at work?" I anticipated this and saw how much fun and engaged everyone was with Babo and Wage, and that it helped us say we had best friends at work and kept the topic alive. We could continue to use Babo and Wage as our unofficial mascots on the topic, and I would love to say that I had an epiphany and figured out how important Best Friends at Work was to our overall culture, driving me to continue working on this with other leaders and my team. But that would be a lie. My motivation at that time was to figure out a way to stop Stan from continuing to ask us, "what are we doing about best friends at work?" and to figure out how to raise that question up from last place on the survey. So, we still had work to do, but what?

I don't want you all to think that from the time that we were introduced to the Gallup Survey in 2014 up until to 2018 that all of this was just me and that we only focused on best friends at work. All leaders participated in this from Stan's senior staff to managers and individual contributors. Culture was something we were taking seriously and there were other areas of the survey each year we focused on and tried to improve on as well. What was great about our entire leadership team is that they embraced culture change, and everyone was determined to make ours the best organization in the company for culture. We did achieve that – because of all our effort on embracing culture and putting people first. We had the #1 culture score two years in a row and tied in year three.

What is unique about that is that within security organizations, it is not really all that common for security folks to embrace culture. Security is usually seen as "enforcers" — the people that show up if you did something wrong and those types of people don't typically embrace the "fluffy culture" stuff. We were not expected to, but I will be the first to tell you, embracing the company's culture will advance your security program and you will see instant benefits.

We understood this as a leadership team and were relentless when it came to improving our culture. It was just this one small annoying question that Stan kept bringing up in staff meetings, "what are we doing about best friends at work"?

"I'm going to do Best Friend Friday," I told Stan. His response was, "okay, what is it?"

# CHAPTER 5

# Best Friend Friday

I STARTED WRITING this chapter a week after the 200th episode of Best Friend Friday (BFF). Now if you have no idea what I am talking about when I say 200th episode or even Best Friend Friday, you're in luck (although you did buy the book, so I'm not sure if luck really played a part here). I will share with you how this began, how it was never intended to go this long, how it had morphed over time into something I never intended it would be, the significance of a stuffed bear, and finally the BFAW (pronounced *Bee-Fawh*).

As I discussed in the previous chapter, at the beginning of our work culture journey there was controversy over the Gallup question "I have a Best Friend at Work," which became the talk of the company. I felt a lot of people, including myself, were overthinking this question and that was a problem. So, I thought to myself, "let's get to the root of the confusion." Most people were getting hung up on the word "best," and when we talked about it further, I think most people agreed that they had friends at work but couldn't honestly state they had a best friend. Merriam-Webster dictionary defines best friends as:

*1: a person's closest and dearest friend.*

Well, that changes things. I had people I worked with that I considered friends. Some I even spent time with outside of work or met with daily and talked about things unrelated to work. I decided that meant I did have Best Friends at work. So Best Friend Friday was born.

Now, I couldn't just write an email explaining my epiphany to everyone. I suppose I could have, but that is boring, and I like to have fun. What better way than to seek out people I considered my best friends and record us together while I asked them what best friends at work meant to them? On a Friday morning in 2018 BFF was born.

I would love to tell you that one night as I slept, a tiny stuffed bear came to me in a dream and spoke to me and that when I woke up, I had the idea of recording videos every Friday with my best friends. That's not exactly what happened, but I do have dreams about bears from time to time. Okay, way off topic... Actually the "concept" of recording people each week and posting the videos came from Scott McGohan, Co-Chairman of McGohan Brabender.

I met Scott at a community meeting in Columbus in 2018 and connected with him on LinkedIn. Every Thursday, Scott posts a video on LinkedIn with him and other people from both inside and outside of his company. These 1–2-minute videos and the posts are called #thankfulthursdays. He is just thanking people for who they are what they do. It's short, simple and he's never missed Thursday.

I honestly can't say when he started doing this, but I was so impressed. Here is the head of a company doing this every Thursday randomly on his own. You can tell from the videos that they are not scripted. I wondered to myself how his employees must have reacted when he first started doing this. The head of the company, showing up wherever you are and recognizing you for a few minutes. I began to think about the power a CEO of a company has, and how just showing up at someone's desk and thanking them for what they do could go a long way. I thought of our CEO at the time, walking the floors once a week and connecting with the employees. How would I react if that happened? The CEO has such an impact on the company as a whole and they could literally change the lives of the workforce with one single action.

I thought of Scott and how he did just that by showing up every Thursday and doing a video with his employees or other individuals to say, "thank you." How simple is that? If Scott can take time out of his day running the entire company to do this, what the hell was I waiting for? I had everything I needed: a phone, a platform, a reason, but what should I call it?

I have a thing for acronyms for some odd reason. I'm not sure why, but I like coming up with acronyms for programs or teams, or even titles. Sometimes you can have fun with them. I knew I wanted to do a recording like Scott, and he already had a good catch phrase for it, #thankfulthursday. Like a lightning bolt, BFF came to me quickly. BFF is most commonly means "Best Friend Forever." It seemed obvious to me to do my videos on Fridays and call it "Best Friend Friday." So, off I went to record my very first BFF video with Emily Moses, where I asked the question that would continue for many more episodes, "what does best friends mean to you?" I also asked why she felt people struggled with that question.

That very first video was 1 minute and nine seconds in length. It was raw, poorly shot (by me), and honestly, I had no idea what I was doing. As I look back on this video, having recorded more than 200 videos since then, whenever I am asked what my favorite BFF episode is, I will always say that it was the first one. I think it's one of my favorites because it was something brand new — I had no idea where it would go from there, there was no pressure on me to put videos out every week, and honestly the expectations were so low if I stopped no one would really care. When I compare that episode to any of the current videos, I reflect on the progress, the people, and then I think about the future.

"So, I have my video, now what?" I thought the easiest way to get this out was to email it to the whole organization at work. That is exactly what I did. I sent an email to our department distribution list and attached the video, introducing the very first Best Friend Friday. I don't really recall the reactions and never did save the original email, but I knew one thing — if this was going to make any impact, it had to be done regularly, every Friday. I had no idea how people would take it and even if people would care, but to get anything accomplished you must be relentless in your actions, and I knew I had to find my next best friend to feature.

Over the next several weeks, I continued to connect with best friends in our department, ask them pretty much the same question each time and post the videos. I started getting feedback from our team with people responding to the email, or when they saw me in the hallways. It seemed that people were enjoying them, but I bet most people were probably thinking this was just another fad. I never made a big announcement that we would be doing these all year.

We, as the organization leadership team, decided everyone should start doing these as well, so we started featuring my counterparts in Security and our leader Stan connecting with an employee in our department to record BFF episodes. I continued to do them, so for the first year of BFF I wasn't doing every single episode, which was never my real intent. I just wanted to spread the message that we all do have best friends at work and to use Fridays as that reminder.

Soon other teams started making a BFF video and sending them to me for distribution. It even turned into a little competition among teams, and we got some amazing videos that first year. That was a lot of fun, because the teams were getting really creative, doing themes, dressing up, using props and making the videos a lot longer and funnier all while showcasing their best friends at work. We never stopped promoting Babo and Wage and we continued to receive photos during this time of team members taking pictures of themselves and family members with Babo and Wage.

It was evident that we were really focusing on our culture and putting forth the effort as an organization to make this a priority. I was truly amazed at what everyone had done, and it worked because at the end of 2018 our culture scores had gone up and we had the #1 culture score in the entire company. I know a survey is nothing more than a measuring tool, but heck, we really enjoyed being number one. For a Security organization to be leaders in a company's culture is pretty rare in my opinion, because most security organizations are viewed as costly and as enforcers, always telling people what they can and can't do. We didn't want to be viewed that way, so we embraced the culture shift and gained much success because of it.

Early on in our culture journey, we formed a Culture Committee of individual contributors and managers from the Security organization. This team was charged with coming up with ideas and initiatives to focus on culture for our organization. The Culture Committee asked me if they could take on Best Friend Friday and continue what we did the prior year, but this year they wanted to not only feature our own team members but connect with a few people outside of Security. I willingly agreed and encouraged them to go for it!

As they started putting out the videos, I would be lying if I said that I was totally happy with the outcome. The videos were good, don't get me wrong, and I know that when you turn control of something over to another group you must give them the freedom to learn. But what frustrated me the most was that videos were not coming out every Friday, they were only coming out when the Culture Committee found time to do them. I kept my frustrations to myself because I didn't want to discourage the team, but inside I felt that BFF was MY BABY, and they were screwing it up. Again, I knew intellectually that they were not doing anything wrong, and I was happy they wanted to do it, but I felt Best Friend Friday could be more than what they were doing. There were so many times I wanted to go to them and say, hey you're screwing this up, you need to do it this way or that way. I never did that, I wanted them to have total freedom to do it their way. I could have met with them and asked them if they wanted my help, but I did not because I wanted to give them full control.

At one point in 2019 the videos stopped with no explanation. They take work and I get that, but it just ended. I didn't get angry because they stopped and, I didn't even ask why. Best Friend Friday had run its course and that was fine. It wasn't meant to last more than a year and after it ended in 2018, we were technically done. We hadn't given up on our culture efforts, we continued to work on other things, and I focused on other culture actions as well. However, when the BFF videos stopped, the idea never left my mind, and I continued silently to think about Best Friend Friday.

I cannot tell you exactly when, but at some point, in 2019, I thought to myself, "next year I am taking back Best Friend Friday." I enjoyed doing them, and I wanted to "own" them again, but this time with a little twist. We would not feature anyone from Security because I wanted to connect with people outside of the Security organization. Up until that point, all videos were recorded in the headquarters building in Columbus, OH, because that is where most of the Security team worked.

In my role, I travel to all over our service territories often and meet a lot of people in different departments and at different levels in the company. I thought it would be great to feature them each week, and ask the same question I had been asking, "What does a best friend mean to you?" and ask them who their best friend is at work. This way I could tag that person in the email when I sent out the video. My hope was that it could catch on and people would begin forwarding the email to others. Another way I thought I could reach more people with the videos was to post them on LinkedIn. I posted the first few videos of me in 2018, but as the other leaders began making them, I didn't post them on LinkedIn. At that time, I didn't use LinkedIn much and didn't have many followers, but I thought it would be a good way to reach more people. Another idea I thought might keep people engaged was to wear a different funny t-shirt for each episode that had something to do with best friends. You would be amazed at how many T-shirts are out there with that theme. My goal was to have a different t-shirt for each episode (no repeats!), so it was Amazon to the rescue.

*Me with David Ball wearing the first BFF t-shirt (Season 3 Episode 1)*

Now that I was determined to take on Best Friend Friday and had somewhat of a "plan" to roll this out, I was ready to get started in January of 2020. Now, I am using the word "plan" very lightly because I had no formal plan or a list of people I was going to connect with, and I thought this would be easy to do. As I went to work or traveled to a building, I would just find someone and say to them, let's record a BFF. Let's just say there were a few flaws in that "plan." The first challenge was that no one knew what the heck Best Friend Friday was. I knew I could post the videos easily on LinkedIn, but what about people that are not on LinkedIn? I would still need to get the videos on the company network to email them out. Another challenge was the effort and consistency needed to record and share the videos every week. I wanted to make sure I had a diverse group of people at all levels of the company and in all different roles – I wanted to showcase all of "the people" at AEP. Another challenge I had was my actual day job with other work and responsibilities, BFF was definitely not part of my full-time job.

I had to fit recording and processing the videos on my own time. Obviously, I recorded the videos at work but taking on additional work doesn't mean that other work just stops. I didn't let these minor challenges deter me though, I honestly didn't think it was a big deal and since I really didn't commit to doing the videos or make some grand announcement that I was going to restart BFF. I thought no one would care if I stopped, and there was no pressure except for from myself – I just needed to DO IT. The other motivating factor for me was a statement Shelene Bryan, former Hollywood producer and founder of Skip1.org, made at an event I attended. She said, "I'm not worried you are going to fail at anything, my fear is you might succeed at something that doesn't matter." This statement and her story about how she gave everything up to start her non-profit really stuck with me. What was I doing in my life that mattered? How could BFF really make a difference, could it make people care more about others? Could we focus on best friends and making relationships better? Could I, Sam Queeno, really make an impact on the culture at my company? Would what I was about to set out to do really matter to anyone? I had no clue, but I knew I wanted to spread the message that we all had best friends, especially at work, and having best friends allows you to be a better person. It is my belief that best friends working together can change the world. How much better this world would be if we all had best friends?!

With my mind made up, and somewhat of a plan, I called my Best Friend Dave Ball. I told him what I wanted to do and asked if he would be in the first video. I first met Dave, who is now Senior Vice President in our Energy Delivery organization, through various work meetings. I never knew Dave outside of work, but because of our personalities, we became friends and made each other laugh, joking around and playing jokes on each other. This is what happens organically when you are at work. Working around other people, you start making connections and form relationships. This was what

I was hoping to showcase as I set out in 2020 to expel the myth that at work is not a place for making friends (or best friends). Since that video, Dave has been on a few other BFF episodes throughout the years and is a huge supporter of driving positive culture at work.

Well, I was rocking it in 2020, and continued to reach out to other people in the company that I knew and had them on every Friday. I continued to post the videos on LinkedIn and was emailing them out internally to the Security Organization as well as tagging other departmental group emails that the episode "guest" worked for, the best friend they mentioned on the video, and other email groups I was a member of. This was the best way I knew how to get these videos out. When I sent the email, I asked people to forward it on to others to spread the message and make Friday the day we celebrate our Best Friends. I won't lie, a part of me hoped that one day my company really would adopt Friday as Best Friend Friday, and it would be a day we talked about our people and best friends. We do this now somewhat, but not at the level I would love to see it go. That is fine, it just reminds me that WE have more work to do.

January and February seemed to fly by, and because I had committed to put out a video every Friday, it seemed even faster because I kept looking at the next Friday and had to figure out who was going to be on, and where I was going to film. From recording to posting I only had a few days, and let's not forget that this wasn't what the company was actually paying me to do, which was run the Physical Security department that I was responsible for.

And then everything came to a screeching stop when March rolled around and this strange virus, we were hearing about in China became real. Yes, I am talking about COVID and the pandemic. With growing concern around the virus and a potential pandemic, the company prepared to test everyone's remote work capability in case we needed to send everyone home. They sent as many people home as possible to test working remotely. Our HQ building was empty, and I recorded that week's episode with two IT individuals who stayed in the building. The floor we recorded it on normally would have been filled with people working, and it was empty. That Friday, the video went out and the pandemic became a reality – the work from home "test" became permanent.

The order was given for everyone in the company to work from home unless your job required you to be in the field or your work could not be performed from home. Right then and there, I knew Best Friend Friday was over. With no people physically at work, there was no one I could record. On top of that, we were in the middle of a global pandemic. We had a lot more important things to be concerned with than with putting out a BFF video. The world was essentially shut down and our buildings became ghost towns. Literally, at our HQ building there was me, our contract security force, and some janitorial and maintenance personnel. All travel was suspended, and we needed to focus on this pandemic.

"Why don't you just do BFF virtually?" That is what my best friend Frank Ginocchi, who at the time was Director of Safety & Health at AEP, asked me. My first response was, "Heck no, I hate these virtual meetings," which were all we were doing, and I had no idea how I would do a virtual "BFF" video. Now I look back and laugh at that. How many times in life are we unable to see any alternatives because we are too close to the issue at hand? Sometimes at work and in life you need to step back and see the problem from a different perspective. Sometimes in life you need your best friend to help you with a problem, even if you don't ask for help.

Frank knew how much I liked doing BFF, he was a supporter and probably saw how it could be impactful. Frank recommended that I use my iPad and FaceTime to connect with the person. I could then record the video of me talking to the person on the iPad. Now I know there is probably a better technical way to do this, but I didn't want to it feel like a "Zoom Call" (that is what everyone was

calling those back then even if we didn't use Zoom). So, I got a stand
for the iPad and then got someone from the Security team to record
me talking to the person who can be seen on the iPad. It looked like
a studio interview with the host on set and the guest on the screen.
It was grainy with poor video quality because it was a video recording of a video, and I had no special microphones set up. After I or-
dered what I needed to make it happen, I told Frank I would do it,
but he needed to be my first guest in this new format. He suggested
that I do it to look like he was in his office behind his desk but on my
iPad. We tried that first, but the network connection was horrible,
so we moved to another area in the building, and we recorded the
first virtual BFF.

With the new virtual BFF logistics somewhat figured out, I
pressed on and started reaching out to people asking them to be on
BFF. The beauty of being in a 31-story building with no people was
that I could go anywhere in the building and have all the privacy
I needed to record. With a new T-shirt every week, I decided to
sprinkle in wearing costumes as well to surprise the guests and start
making people laugh. I would dress up periodically for the episodes
to bring some humor to the videos. I had always dreamed of working as a mascot or Disney character, so putting on a costume was
right up my alley. I wanted to have fun doing these and make sure
the word would spread that we all had best friends at work.

As the weeks turned into months and the pandemic was not
ending any time soon, more and more places closed, but BFF was
open for business. I continued to have people on in their makeshift
offices at home, their hair growing longer since we couldn't even get
out for a haircut, and every Friday without fail I asked each person,
"What does having a Best Friend mean to you?" My email distribution list continued to grow as I tried to share BFF with as many
people as I could, asking each of them every week to forward it on
to their best friend at work.

To wrap up the 2020 season, I even managed to have on some executives, including our CEO Nick Akins for the holiday finale. In true Nick fashion, he surprised me when I FaceTime him. He told me he wanted kick it off by playing drums, and that he had the perfect song ready. So, we hit record, I introduced him, and he began to play "You're my Best Friend" by Queen. He played the first verse, and then sat down so I could ask him that same question I had been asking everyone all year. This episode was not scripted. I had no idea he was planning to do this, but when I reached out to his administrative assistant several months earlier, I simply asked if he would be on BFF and if he could play his drums. I was amazed that he said yes. The best part was that I hadn't told a soul he was going to be on – I just recorded it and sent it out. It was amazing to have him on and for the first time that year, I really thought we had something special. I mean, I had our CEO on BFF and all I had to do was ask. I was on cloud nine and so proud of what was accomplished that year.

A couple of months before the Holiday episode, I was talking to people within the company about a better way to save the videos and distribute them. Because I had been emailing the videos to people as an attachment, a few things happened. One issue was that the videos had to be a certain size, or they wouldn't send, and the second issue was that the videos were filling up space in everyone's inboxes, which only had a limited capacity. So, if you had a full email inbox already and I sent you a BFF email on Friday, you could exceed your allotted capacity and wouldn't get any more emails until you cleaned it up. I found out some people were not deleting the emails after they viewed them, which continued to take up space. We tried several different solutions for storing the videos internally and sharing a link to the video in the email instead. As we played through the logistics on how this worked, I got a call that changed everything, and made BFF even more legit.

A best friend in our corporate communication department called to tell me that I once again shut down his email inbox because of the size of the videos. I said, "Yes I know, and I am trying to work out a solution." His response to that was, "Well why don't you just put them on AEP TV and create a blog?" He said it in a way that sounded so simple to him, but I thought to myself, "Okay, how the heck do I do that?" AEP TV is an internal site where all corporate communication videos are posted. To me, it seemed like getting the videos posted there, where they would continue to live forever would make BFF a legitimate initiative. He offered to ask if it could be done and would work on getting me access to it. After a few short weeks, I was given access and an internal blog to post BFF each Friday, which coincided with the kickoff of Season 4. Now I needed to upgrade my recording capability, which was simply buying a large monitor to display the person via FaceTime and a microphone for better audio quality, and then we were rolling!

With season 4, I began learning to incorporate different things in the videos, and I introduced "Sammy Bear." The idea behind Sammy Bear was to try and get people to subscribe to our internal blog. I was obsessed with getting those numbers up, so weekly we would randomly select a subscriber to win the Sammy Bear. Over time, this evolved into asking our guests on BFF who they want to give a Sammy Bear too. I also started giving them to people at random or because they had done something special to be a best friend. I felt it was needed to continue to spread the message about Best Friend Friday, get people talking about their best friends, and keep it on everyone's mind. The Sammy Bear thing was a lot like our journey early on with Babo and Wage. By giving you a Sammy Bear, I was giving you a Best Friend, but more importantly a Best Friend wanted you to have this stuffed bear because they value you as being special to them.

The main thing to remember about the Best Friend Friday videos is that they are not scripted, never really planned, and 99% of the time the guest has no idea what I am going to say. A few of them may know the theme prior to the recording, such as the holiday episodes, but most of the time when our guest star accepts the FaceTime call from me, they will see me in a costume, t-shirt, or hat and I'll kick things off with the standard question about best friends. Over the years, the standard question has changed slightly based on the challenge we get from our Chief Human Resource Officer.

Each Thanksgiving I ask our CHRO about what challenge he gives everyone related to being a best friend. In 2022, the challenge was to go out and meet a new best friend at work. So, in Season 5, I asked each guest if they could tell me about any new best friends, they met this year.

The hardest part of continuing to do these each year is keeping them fresh and different. I don't sit there and plan out each week, ideas will just come to me during the episode, or the person that I have on makes the episode amazing because of something they do. Again, none of this is really planned or scripted, it just happens naturally, which I think makes it easier for people to relate. Over the years, Best Friend Friday has morphed into more than the weekly videos. It has started to become a movement where we recognize having best friends not only at my company but also from outside of my company.

The videos became the driver (or the "HOW") of how we get the word out, but the "WHY" is much bigger, and that is what we are striving for. If more people connect with others and become best friends, this world would be a better place. A safer place, a world where anything is possible. We cannot accomplish anything alone, and having best friends to help you achieve your goals makes them possible.

I don't have a team of people that work on BFF, but I am not a one man show. There are many people that do their part to make this possible each week. From someone pressing the record button, to corporate communication helping me when there is an issue with a video, the many BFF champions that repost the videos and send messages of encouragement to me or share about having best friends at work. It also includes my company leadership, who allow me to do this, the people who have made content suggestions, the amazing BFAW guests who give me their wisdom and have fun while I interview them, the people that I have connected with who understand what I am trying to do and encourage others to connect, and that one individual that decides they are going to meet someone new today and become best friends at work. This is how something like BFF gets done – it is not one person; it is a community of best friends. It is this community that is going to make Best Friend Friday into something that is yet to be imagined. The future of BFF is unknown, which I am fine with because I know it will become something if it is meant to be. I will only get closer to knowing what it could become as each Friday passes and we continue to spread the word that we all have best friends at work.

*Scott McGohan, Co-Chairman of McGohan Brabender with me doing a virtual BFF.*
*Scott was the very first guest from outside AEP to participate in BFF.*
*(Season 4 Episode 17)*

# CHAPTER 6

# The BFAW Concept

I AM BLOWN away when I hear from someone how much seeing BFF each Friday helped them during the pandemic or brings a smile to their face every Friday. As I let you know in the previous chapter, BFF celebrated its 200th episode. The 200th episode aired June 8th, 2023, and it featured "Sammy Bear" hosting the show (I was dressed up in a life size bear costume) interviewing a lot of Best Friends who shared with us the identity of their best friend at work. A month later the company ran a featured story on our internal website celebrating the 200th episode. It was so humbling to see that article and to read the comments. It was a proud moment for me in my career and for BFF, but what people don't know is that over the six seasons of doing BFF, I have learned more than anyone could imagine. I have benefited the most out of everyone and still do today because of the people I connect with each week and what BFF has become because of the people that support it and spread the message. BFF has allowed me to meet with people that I may not have crossed paths with but more importantly the people I have met or those who have been guests on BFF each week have provided wisdom on being a best friend that I morphed into what I like to call the BFAW concept.

Yes, I know BFAW really stands for Best Friend At Work. Like many things on BFF, I was not the one that originally came up with the acronym. I can't remember exactly, but one of our guests either introduced BFAW to me or shared it as a message at the end of the video (I always give the guest the parting words). I had heard it before in passing at work in conversations about best friends, but this episode was the first time I got the chance to officially introduce it. After the episode aired, we naturally just started to adopt this term when referring to our best friends in the workplace. Since BFF technically no longer stood for Best Friend Forever in our little world.

While I'm on the topic of sharing wisdom from our guests on Season 6, David Robinson, gave us his THE philosophy he uses when describing having best friends. David says the first thing you need to have with your best friend is **TRUST**. You need to have trust amongst each other at all times. The second part is **Honesty**, you need to have honesty between each other. You need to have someone that can tell you when to pull back or push forward. We need honesty because we all have faults. The last letter in his philosophy E stood for **Empathy**. You need to have the ability to understand each other and share our feelings. David believes this is what we all should strive for in being best friends.

So, what is the BFAW concept? It is the simplest, easy to adapt concept that is out there, but it can be very impactful. Honestly, it is something we should be doing already in our lives and probably do but don't realize. However, because of all the wisdom I have gained from meeting with people and really paying attention to what best friends mean to everyone, I felt the need to describe to others what this morphed into and how we got here. Now this is not a "how to" become a best friend at all. It is not a roadmap that will explain exactly what you need to do to instantly become a best friend to someone. What this concept will do is to help you connect with the other humans in your life because guess what, we are better when we have best friends in our lives.

## BFAW

### Better Relationships
### Fun
### Action
### Why

When I introduce this concept to people, I like to describe it backwards because you need the last part to get to the first part. Confused yet? Good, it is my intention to have some fun with you. Should we start with Fun? Nope, we start with WHY. So, when I am describing the concept, I like to start with WHY — actually your WHY.

So WHY = Action + Fun x Better Relationships. Now we have a formula that has no real meaning, so let's begin talking about this nutty concept that I came up with and live by in my life. I figured if I threw it into a formula, it would look pretty cool and maybe someone could try and figure it out for me.

Let's begin with your WHY. Why did you get out of Bed this morning? Why did you choose to show up today at work? What is your Why? As I told you, the Why is the first concept in BFAW but at the end of the acronym. I believe this is the first thing you must figure out before you can do anything in this world. Now there have been many books, training and talks on finding your Why. My hero Simon Sinek has done much work on this topic, including books, videos, and training. So, by no means is the W in the BFAW concept anything new or earth shattering. What it is though is a reminder that to get anything done on this earth you need to figure out why you are here.

If the WHY concept is foreign to you, you may have heard it described as your "Noble Goal," or "North Star." There are probably many names for it, but in simplest terms I always like to say it is the reason you get out of bed every day. The WHY is not just for individuals, but I think it needs to start there. There could be the WHY for a particular team, or organization, or a company. Many translate this to their "mission." Our Security organization developed our WHY, which gets repeated daily on our morning call by one of our team members when we ask the following:

"Who wants to give us our why this morning?"

Then someone goes on to say,

> "*We aspire to be better than our best by owning our mission to protect people, information, assets and our customers' way of life through proactively making safety, compliance, and reliability driving factors in our security program.*"

This WHY was for our organization, and to get there we asked everyone to come up with what they thought should get us out of bed each morning. We then took parts of what people said and our WHY was born.

It is great to have a WHY for your team or organization, but what about YOU as a person? What is it that drives you, what are you all about, what is your WHY? It can be a struggle to know where to begin. It can be difficult to figure out your WHY and it may take many years. I believe Your WHY can change over time as you change as a person. However, your WHY is infinite, it never ends. You will not complete it in your lifetime, you will continue striving each day to live out your WHY until you die.

An example is my WHY, which took quite a while to define and redefine. My WHY is *"striving to make the world a safer place to live, work and play."* That is why I get out of bed each morning. You may think this only has to do with Security, my current profession, but that is just one component. Your WHY is not necessarily the profession you work in (however it helps if they are aligned). Your WHY is more than a job.

In my WHY, "safer" does mean exactly what you think because I work in Security, but that is not all. What about being kind to someone or being there to just listen to a friend in need. Could that make them feel safe? Is Best Friend Friday in line with my WHY? I am pretty sure it is and that is why I do it. If you don't know where to even start, I came up with a simple idea for you to consider.

We call it the 3 P's.

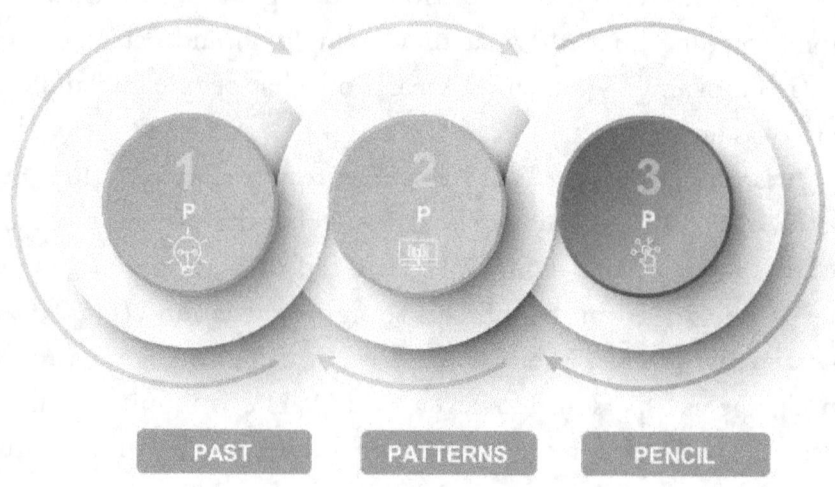

**Past** – Look at what you have done in the past. Talk with your Best Friends and ask them why they are friends with you. Getting an understanding of you as a person is the first step.

**Patterns** – As you begin to think of your past and talk with your friends, you will organically start seeing patterns in your life. What is the same about you over time?

**Pencil** – Now it is time to grab your pencil and start writing out your why. Write down all that you have explored, what your friends said about you, and draft your why. I like using a pencil instead of a pen because a pencil is not permanent and your WHY can be easily adjusted.

The one thing I want you to take away from this chapter is to get started. Doing nothing will give you the same results you have now, and you will never get to your WHY. Commit to figuring out your WHY by any means necessary. Again, I am not the expert in this, I have just taken what I've learned and talked with my best friends to help me refine and come up with the WHY I live by every day. This is my personal brand and what defines me. It's my trademark, and since I am so serious about it, I actually did have it trademarked. My WHY is my sole purpose in life, and what I want to be remembered for when I am gone. I continue to ask myself every day if I am living my WHY.

Continuing our backwards reading of the BFAW concept, let's talk about Action. I introduced you to Action back in chapter 3. If you're like me, you probably have forgotten chapter 3 by now, so let me remind you or… SLAP you, so you can remember. SLAP stands for Serve Love Action Passion. This is what I live by as a leader. The A in SLAP stands for action and I will continue to stress that you need to take action to accomplish anything. So many people simply talk about doing something, or come up with reasons why something cannot happen, but how many of us really take action?

It seems like such a simple concept, but I bet every single one of us has discussed something or has wanted to do something and then has failed to take action. There could be a number of reasons for the inaction, and I am not here to judge. There could be very valid reasons why there is inaction on your part and only you know why. However, the BFAW concept requires taking any action, and regardless of whether you succeed or not, at least you took action. The outcome may have not been the desired result but that should not stop you from taking action. The fear of failure is very powerful, so powerful that it encourages inaction on our part. "Fear is the path to the dark side" (another Yoda quote for you). Yoda also says, "fear leads to anger, anger leads to hate, hate leads to suffering." These are all bad things when you consider all you need to do is take action.

With Best Friend Friday, I took the action to just start, and I put a video out. I also took action to reach out to people and ask them to be on BFF, like when I reached out to our CEO, Nick. The worst that could happen was that he could say no, but at least

I tried. I thought to myself, "What is the worst thing that could happen with putting out BFF?" I was doing something that was not already being done. The reason BFF is still going strong today is because I continue to take action to put something out each Friday. If I stopped, would it continue? Would someone else pick up where I left off? Time will tell, but for now I will continue to take action.

I like using Newton's third law to explain action. I think about this in life and especially when thinking about being a best friend. If you recall your school lessons, Newton's third law is:

For every action, there is an equal and opposite reaction.

That means that in every interaction, there is a pair of forces acting on the two interacting objects. For those of you who skipped this lesson, in a nutshell, it means when you sit in a chair you are pushing force downward on the chair and the chair is pushing upward on your body. For anything to occur you need to take action, and then what happens next is the reaction. If you do nothing, there is technically no motion, and nothing is getting accomplished.

Let me make this concept even more simple for you. Over the years, people have said to me, "I don't know how to be a best friend to someone at work," or, "Work is not a place to find a long-lasting best friend." My response to them has been to take action and put yourself out there and meet someone. Take my advice literally – while riding in an elevator, introduce yourself to someone and ask them for their name and what team they work on. The greatest thing about being at work is you already have something in common with them. You work for the same company! Now will this first interaction make you instant best friends? No, it will take some time, but you took action to start laying the groundwork until next time. What most people do is remain silent on the elevator – that is inaction.

I continually tell people that Best Friend Friday is bigger than a weekly video, it is about connecting with others and being a best friend to someone. Best Friends can change the world. I truly believe that, but it requires action by someone. The concept teaches us that by connecting and taking action you can accomplish anything you want. We cannot achieve our goals alone, so what better way but to have Best Friends to help you. The more Best Friends you have, the more that can be accomplished. As I look back at anything that I've accomplished, there was at least one person that helped me accomplish whatever I was doing. It could have been something minor, but there was a connection with someone else that gave me what I was seeking.

To sum up the A in BFAW, it is the driving force of getting anything accomplished and how you show up every day. It sounds so simple, but too many of us do not take that first step. Be the driving force to push others to accomplish something. Having or being a Best Friend not only can be the driving force for someone, but you can also be the person that takes the action to accomplish the goal.

Now let's have some fun! The next part of our concept is Fun. Now before you get too excited, there is no way I can teach you how to have fun, so this section may end up being very short. What I can do is talk about the importance of Fun in the BFAW concept. If you google how much time people spend at work during their lifetime, you will see so many articles and studies that estimate that the average person will spend **one-third** of their life at work. That's roughly **90,000 hours** at work over your lifetime.

So, let me ask you, wouldn't it be nice if a portion of those hours were filled with fun and laughter? The main reason Fun was included in the BFAW concept is because most people (I hope) have fun with their best friends. I will be first to say that especially at work, life can't be and isn't **always** fun. However, anytime we have the ability to have fun we need to do it. Life can be too serious, and if we are spending one-third of our life at work, we MUST, and I'll say it again, we MUST have fun.

My current position as a Director in our Corporate Security department, requires me (in most instances) to be a "serious guy." That makes perfect sense given what I am responsible for and what I must get involved in, and that is when I need to turn on serious Sam. However, at heart I am a fun, loving guy that wants to make people laugh. I want to have fun at work, and I try to encourage it because the byproduct is happier people and a more engaged workforce. I am sure many of you have worked for companies that made you dread showing up and you just couldn't wait until it was time to leave for the day.

The Best Friend Friday videos are all about having fun and having great banter with our guests. Some of my most memorable BFF videos are with our Senior Leaders in the company who were having fun with their 3-4 minutes of fame on BFF. I was able to interview some very serious leaders, but because they knew what we were trying to accomplish, they showed their true personalities on camera. It showed our leaders in a different light and that is what people want to see.

Fun cannot be forced. Forced Fun, is the worst Fun, meaning you shouldn't make it mandatory to have your teams show up at a local establishment to throw axes because you feel that is the only way to build a team. Fun should just come naturally by having a mindset of how you choose to show up. What I have found over the years working with adults is that there is a kid inside each of us dying to come out and play.

If you walk into our team conference room at the office it is filled with toys like Mr. Potato Head, Stretch Armstrong, Etch a Sketch, Pac-Man, Slinky, and much more. It puts people at ease and adults want to play. This is how I got the idea of "Sammy Bear."

Think about how many of us have gone to one of the Disney Parks as an adult and the minute you walk through the gates and see Mickey, you instantly get excited and turn into a 7-year-old kid again. I hoped that these small stuffed bears with a red hoodie would allow people to have some fun with them. I have had people take pictures with them, put them on their desks, take them to dinner and much more. They are having fun, and Sammy is a reminder to us that it is alright to carry a stuffed animal around with you because it may make someone smile. (Yes, I have a Sammy Bear in my work bag at all times.)

*Sammy Bear*

People also love free t-shirts, me included. It is one of my weird obsessions. I love it when you're given free "swag" at a conference or some promotional item at an event you are attending. I always say the goofier an item is, the better. I had my best friend Brian Wheatley from LeaderPromos in Columbus, Ohio, help me create some unique swag for Best Friend Friday. So now we have t-shirts, hats, mugs, and of course Sammy Bear with the BFF logo on them.

You cannot buy them and even though I have been asked, they are exclusive items I only give away to Best Friends. It serves two purposes really. One, I just want to give my Best Friend a gift. There is nothing special you have to do to earn one, I randomly give them to people, or if someone asks for one and has seen an episode or makes a comment, I will send them one. This is fun for me and just a small token to keep the Fun concept going. The second purpose, which I love when it happens, is they actually wear them out or post a picture with them on. It puts people in the right frame of mind to act a little bit differently when engaging with others.

They are spreading the BFF message when they do this, and hopefully someone will ask them about it while they're wearing it. For those that don't understand the logo, interlocked index fingers are the American Sign Language for "Friend." I want to spread the message that we all have best friends at work and want people to accept the challenge and ask what they are doing to be a best friend to someone.

So, is the concept telling you that this is the only way to have Fun? NO not at all. Don't assume if you go out and buy a ping pong table you will have an instantly fun environment and that people are going to run back to the office. A ping pong table is just a tool for you. If your company treats everyone like a number and it's not fun to be working there or to be working for you, all you've done is waste your money on a piece of furniture. You have to find what works for you and what works with your company's culture. If you work for a company that doesn't have Fun as part of the fabric, refer back to the A in our BFAW concept and take ACTION. One person (you!) can change the culture and make a difference.

So now we have made it to the B in BFAW. You are figuring out your WHY, you are committing to take ACTION in anything you want to accomplish, and you're all about having FUN. So, are you ready to master the hardest part of the concept? Better Relationships! Spoiler alert, if you've got FAW down, Better Relationships is going to come easy to you as long as you put in the effort. There are eight words that I believe are powerful and can help us be better humans. They are attributes I choose to live by. I have carried around a little post-it-note with these words written on it for the last 8 years - I am pretty sure I picked that idea up from a book I was reading at the time, but it stuck with me. These are simple words we all have heard before, and I think if we live by them, we can naturally have better relationships. These words continue to push me daily to show up and are how I want to engage with people to make my relationships with others better. I said "continue to push" because no one is perfect, and sometimes I screw up, but the important part is that I try.

I like to call them the 8 traits to relate. Patience, Kindness, Humility, Respectfulness, Selflessness, Forgiveness, Honesty, and Commitment.

Let's see how Merriam-Webster dictionary defines each of these.

**Patience** – the capacity, habit, or fact of being patient

**Kindness** – the quality or state of being kind

**Humility** – freedom from pride or arrogance; the quality or state of being humble

**Respectfulness** – marked by or showing respect or deference

**Selflessness** – having no concern for self; UNSELFISH

**Forgiveness** – the act of forgiving

**Honesty** – adherence to the facts; SINCERITY; fairness and straightforwardness of conduct

**Commitment** – an agreement or pledge to do something in the future

I will be the first to admit, I suck at patience. I am not by nature a patient person and I strive to get better in that area of my life. I know this is one of my faults, and knowing is half the battle. Being patient with people will definitely help you have better relationships. It will also reduce your own stress if you can lead in with patience.

For example, what if your best friend has reached out to you time and time again telling you they want to leave their job because they hate what they do? You give them the advice you think is best, but they take no steps to change the environment they are in. They come back to you time and time again, complaining about the same issue and say they want to leave, and you continue to provide the advice, but your patience is running thin, and you are tired of them not taking action. This is where you need extra patience because you love your friend and want them to be happy, but they are not ready to make a change. You need to have patience and talk with them to understand more. It may seem simple to you because you were the one that gave them the advice, but to them it's not so simple. So, you need to have patience.

Another example I struggle with is email. I get annoyed when I don't get a response to an email I send. I try to ensure I respond to every email I get daily to at least acknowledge I received it and read it. What I don't understand is how people can simply never respond and require you to send two or three follow ups. This irks me to no end. But if I truly want to have better relationships, it does me no good to send a nasty email pointing out that someone has ignored me for the last three weeks. First, I have no idea what may be going on with this person, and I need to assume positive intent before I respond. What I am trying to point out is that if you are a patient person, there are better ways to handle situations like this for both you and your relationship with others. My approach is always to try and kill them with kindness!

Welcome to the Kindness games! This was started by two BFAWs I met through mutual friends because of Best Friend Friday. Lee Oughton and Tim Wenzel, two amazing Security professionals co-founded The Kindness games: **https://thekindnessgames. com/**. The Kindness Games is something we should all be doing regularly, but these two amazing humans took it to another level. The Kindness Games were created in September of 2020 and started as a way to counter the disruption, hate, and the disconnect that engulfed the world during the COVID-19 pandemic. Lee and Tim aim to heal relationships and communities through targeted kindness. Their unique take on spreading kindness and challenging others to do the same is their way of making the world a better place.

Being a kind person is really a no brainer in my opinion, but unfortunately some do struggle with being kind. Obviously if you are attempting to connect with people to become best friends, if you're not being kind, good luck with that! I tend to try and avoid unkind people, but if I have to engage with them, I try to treat them with grace and kindness because as Ian MacLaren once said (though it's widely attributed to Plato), "Be kind, for everyone you meet is fighting a hard battle."

According to my trusty Merriam-Webster dictionary, relationships "are the way in which two or more concepts, objects, or people are connected, or the state of being connected." As we try to make better relationships, I believe that at least one person in that relationship should practice humility, if not both. I think people tend to forget how powerful it is to be humble. Being humble requires us to put others' needs before our own. I think this is key in relationships. Make sure you are aware of your own shortcomings, strengths, and limitations. Then use your best friend to help you with these items. Open your ears, close that mouth, and be a good listener, make sure others feel heard. Practicing humility is key to becoming a better person and to having better relationships.

"R-E-S-P-E-C-T find out what it means to me." The late, great Aretha Franklin knew a lot about respectfulness. The Golden Rule is to do unto others as you would have them do unto you. We need to respect each other, period! In this world, the problem is that we don't respect each other's opinions or beliefs and are too quick to judge. Be better than that and make this world a better place, even if it is not reciprocated.

If you do that, now you're practicing selflessness, look at you! Now I know the definition of selflessness states "having no concern for self," but I wouldn't take that too literally, because you need to take care of yourself before you can take care of others. Remember, your oxygen mask goes on first before you can help others with their mask. To me, selflessness means putting the needs of others before your own and caring about whether your best friend is okay, even if you are not.

I am a true believer in the power of giving. It is better to give than to receive. That is just not a fluff statement – try it sometime. It is a lot more meaningful to give a gift, whatever that may be, and see the person you care about enjoying it. To have a better relationship, put the people in your life first and watch it boomerang back to you.

If you get hit on the head with that boomerang from your best friend, please forgive them. Forgiveness is hard, I get it. I am not going to lie to you, there are people in my life that have done me wrong, and I have yet to forgive them, so I have no right to tell you to forgive everyone in your life. That would make me a hypocrite. What I will share with you is that person you have yet to forgive probably has no idea you're mad at them or doesn't care, and it's you who needs to let it go. For your own peace of mind, practice forgiving. I promise I will try as well, because if we are really trying to have better relationships, we need to learn to forgive.

Let's be honest. We already talked about Honesty remember? It was what my BFAW Dave Robinson used to describe being a best friend. No need to say anything more on this topic. If you're a dishonest person, good luck with keeping any relationships long term. Honesty is necessary in any relationship and best friends need to be honest with each other no matter what is at stake.

I am committing to end this chapter now, I promise! That is a commitment folks, and the last trait of the eight traits to having better relationships. I like this one the best, because it sums up everything, we have discussed in the BFAW concept. Are you committed to taking this on and practicing being a BFAW? Only you can answer that question.

But **honestly** you have been very **patient** reading this book so far, and it was so **kind** of you to buy the book. Maybe you gave one to your best friend and that shows that you are **selfless. I respect** your opinion regarding the BFAW concept, and in turn hope you will respect me for at least attempting to do this. I am being very **humble** when I say I really don't know what I am doing when it comes to writing a book, and I will listen to any feedback I receive.

The best I can hope for is that you will **forgive** me if you think it sucks. Just do me one favor, if you do anything, **commit** to being the best person you can be. My challenge to you is this question, "What are you doing to be a best friend to someone?"

# CHAPTER 7

# Sammy Bear Challenge

DID YOU THINK Sammy Bear wouldn't get a chapter named after him? He has been an integral part of the journey, so I figured I would name Chapter 7 the Sammy Bear challenge. In reality it is the BFF Challenge, but shhhhhhh I am not telling him that. For my BFAWs reading this book and all the BFF followers, this is a call to action. I hope you picked up some nuggets throughout this book that can help you create your own BFF so we can change the world one best friend at a time.

Am I asking you to start recording your own BFF? Sure, why not, if that is what you want to do. Or am I saying, make a phone call every Friday to one of your best friends and tell them how much you appreciate them? I am guessing you may prefer text since not many people actually "call" anymore. Yes, go for it, text away!

I just gave you two examples of what you could do, but I want you to do you. I want you to figure out what works for you and make a decision to do it. The first thing you need to do is accept the challenge and go for it. Start simply, through how you show up every day and live your life and work your way up to the other stuff if you need to. Remember, you just read about the BFAW concepts, so start going backwards to go forward. You've got two BFAWs to help you along the way. That's me and Sammy Bear in case you were wondering. I am here for you regardless of whether we ever meet or not. If you want to take this challenge and need help, let's connect so I can become your BFAW.

You may be asking yourself why this is so important and why does it really matter? Honestly, I saw the light in the dark cave. If you remember, I was the guy who didn't care much about culture and didn't get personal with the people I led. That all changed because of the many best friends in my life that wanted me to change – that was the original BFF challenge before it was the official BFF challenge.

As I continued the BFF videos each week, it gave me an opportunity to meet so many people and hear why best friends are important to them. I truly listen to the wisdom shared each week as I give the guests the parting words. The laughs we share each Friday and watching how others use BFF each Friday to reach out to their best friends is so meaningful and allows them to put their mark on BFF in their own way. I can tell you all of the people engaged with BFF (and there are thousands involved in one way or another) have made a difference. Even something as simple as a like or comment on a BFF LinkedIn post spreads the message, and maybe just maybe, someone new will see it and accept the challenge as well.

BFF has changed my life. Yes, I said it, it has changed my life. I remember a conversation with my former boss, Steve Swick, who was promoted after Stan retired. I couldn't be happier that Steve was promoted because we were both peers working for Stan and he had been at the leader meetings with Stan where he continued to ask us what we were going to do about the best friend question. I have known Steve for a long time and knew he would be a great boss, BFAW, and supporter of Best Friend Friday. He has been all of that and much more.

I don't recall exactly when we had this conversation, it was definitely during the pandemic but when restrictions were loosening up. During a one-on-one meeting, I can't remember what we were discussing, but I am guessing I was venting about something, and it led me to make a statement to him that I will never forget because of his response. I said, "Oh great, so my legacy in this company is going to be Best Friend Friday," and he said, "Sam that is not a bad thing. People know you as the Security guy, but that is not what defines you, you're doing much more with Best Friend Friday and people notice and you're making a difference." The way he said it to me, made me realize that BFF was part of me, my brand and maybe just maybe it was making a difference. That was one of those "pep" talks I needed at the time probably because of work stress, the pandemic or something else I was dealing with. He helped me realize what was important and at that moment Steve was not being my boss, he was being my best friend.

I truly believe that I have benefited the most from doing BFF. One of the major reasons is the profession I have chosen. As a security professional, I have seen and dealt with the terrible things over the 25+ years I've spent in various roles and at different companies. In those roles I have been exposed to a lot of negative people and situations. Doing Best Friend Friday has been very therapeutic for me — it has given me an outlet to see the best of the best, and to have fun. It has allowed me to meet people both at work and outside of my company that I wouldn't have otherwise ever met.

I have learned so much from each guest on BFF. I love the comments and notes I receive from so many BFAWs after they watch an episode. It is a joy for me to see people post a picture of themselves with a BFF t-shirt on, and it is my BFAWs that recharge my battery. I hope all of you, feel the way I feel by taking that BFF challenge and putting yourself out there and really connecting with best friends. I am here to tell you; you're going to end up benefiting more than the receiver.

I couldn't write a book about BFF and not highlight a few BFAWs for how they accepted the challenge and are living and practicing the BFAW concepts. I am taking a risk by doing this, because I realize I cannot write about everyone, and I don't want to hurt anyone's feelings for leaving them out. That is not my intention at all, so I want to apologize up front and blame Sammy Bear, it's his chapter. Let's call these people Super BFAWs, because I consider them to be super Best Friend Friday supporters and champions of what we are trying to do. I am highlighting these folks because what they have done and continue to do has made a significant impact, and I want to recognize them for their contributions.

First, I want to talk about the winner of the inaugural "Nicholas Bear." This is the big, giant bear given out to someone for truly being a best friend and for living out the BFAW concepts. This was first given out in Season 4 at the finale. Jeanne Sherry won the very first Nicholas Bear. She received it because she blew me away with how she decided to connect with BFAWs. Every BFF episode without fail, Jeanne would email the guest that was on BFF that Friday and tell them something she found special about them or what a great job they did, and if she didn't know the person, she would virtually introduce herself. Jeanne retired as a Vice President in our Energy Delivery organization, and some people that were guests on BFF probably had never gotten a personal email from a Vice President. She always copied me on this email, and told me that I did a great job, sharing encouraging words that kept me going. She always sent me private emails after the episodes as well to tell me how it made her feel and to thank me for doing them. Jeanne did this every week, never missing a week until she retired. Even now, she still engages when she can on LinkedIn, and I love her for it. She is a BFAW for life!

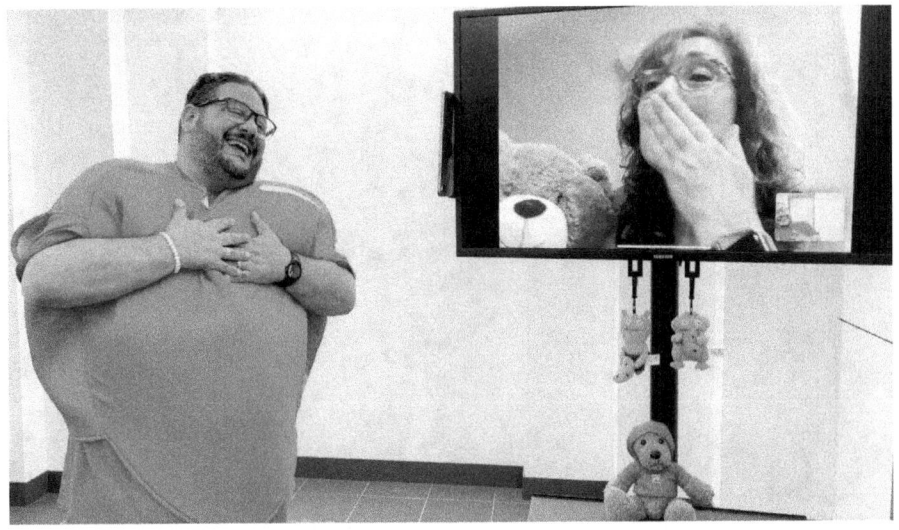

*Jeanne and Nicholas Bear in Season 6 doing BFF before she retired.*

Now on to the Season 5 winner of the Nicholas Bear. This Super BFAW hands down blew everyone else out of the water, and in my opinion is the SUPER DUPER BFAW of all time. I could not write this book without talking about Valerie LeMaster, who at the time worked in my department as a Project Manager. The reason Valerie is the SUPER DUPER BFAW of all time, is because she donated her kidney to her best friend at work, John Anderson. Yes, you read that correctly. Here was an employee with a family and kids that knew her fellow co-worker was in need of kidney, so she got tested, was a match, and donated her kidney to him. I remember when her manager told me this was going to happen. I was speechless, and for me, being speechless is rare. It was an unbelievable act of kindness that gave John the gift of life. They are kidney buddies for life! Her surgery was on a Friday, and yes of course I asked if I could do a BFF from the surgery room, but I was denied by Valerie. Valerie is truly an angel!

*Valerie and John guests on BFF talking about the gift of life.*

*Nick Akins and I announcing Valerie as the Nicholas Bear winner in the Season 5 finale*

I am going go beyond my company BFAWs now and talk about a BFAW I met when I served on a non-profit Board. Christy Bertolo is one of those BFAWs that you may not work with at your place of employment, but because of work you connected in a different arena. When I got to know Christy, I knew she was a rockstar. She is a full-time mom, worked full-time at Ohio State University at the time, volunteered in the community, and did a ton of other stuff for her friends and family.

I was amazed how she did it all, and she never seemed rattled or stressed when I saw her. When our time on the board ended, Christy and I stayed connected. She was an avid follower of Best Friend Friday and one day Christy let me know that she took the leap and left Ohio State to start a business with her BFAW at work from Ohio State Chris Svec. They both worked in the same department and made the decision to become co-founders of UNITE and BridgeED.

As I stated, Christy and I are still BFAWs, and she is the one that has encouraged me to do more with BFF. She convinced me that it wasn't just a video each Friday, that there was more to it. She challenged me to think about how big this could get if I wanted it to grow. She shared her thoughts on how other people who follow BFF outside of my company like her were reacting to it. The creation of the BFAW concepts, the swag, and other fun ideas that are now part of BFF came out of meetings with Christy helping me look at things differently. Her entrepreneurial spirit and thought process have helped make BFF what it is today. She truly was not only a great BFAW to me but has helped me make BFF a brand.

*Christy and Chris on their BFF episode talking about their journey together as BFAWs*

Finally, I cannot end without talking about Stan Partlow, who you know is my person in life. Yes, you have heard a lot about Stan already and what he has done for me and BFF, but what I want to highlight here is how he has been a Best Friend even after he has retired. Sometimes it is the little things we do that could make a difference is someone's life without even knowing about it.

For example, almost every Friday, I can expect a phone call from Stan. If I don't get a call on Friday, it usually means he is traveling or had something come up, but that is rare. If we don't connect on the phone that Friday, it's usually because I cannot pick up. As a retired guy, every day is Saturday for him, but not so much for me yet. If we don't talk on Friday, I will get a text or a voicemail. He calls me to see how things are going because he knows how I feel about Fridays, and we chat about the latest BFF episode.

That is how my BFAW and I stay connected. Now, I talk with Stan throughout the week too, not every day but we do exchange texts or calls. However, his calls or voicemails just to check in on me is an action for a best friend to take. He doesn't need to do that, and you're probably thinking it is a small act and it's not a big deal,

Sam. If you're thinking that, you must have skipped several chapters in this book, because literally that is all it takes. One small act, one action by you can make a difference in someone's life. He chooses to make an effort to connect with me on Friday, because we share BFF in common and he wants to congratulate me on putting out an episode. It means so much to me that he does that each week, and he is relentless in doing it!

*Stan in a BFF episode after he retired, we had him back for a special Star Wars Day BFF*

These are just some examples of ways these Super BFAWs are living the BFAW concepts. I am not saying you need to go out and donate your kidney, but hell, Valerie did, so go for it if you are so inclined, there is no greater gift than the gift of life. My hope is that we all can use BFF to be better humans to each other and be a best friend to someone.

What is the alternative to being a best friend to someone? Being a person that dies without meaningful relationships, leaving this world no better than when you entered it? On your death bed, what is going to matter? Will it be how much money you made, or that big house you purchased, or the fancy car? None of that matters. You cannot take any of the stuff with you. What is going to matter is how you lived your life and what people remember about you. What was your lasting impact on this world? The day you were born, the clock started ticking down to the end. Some of us have more time on the clock than others, but time is precious and shouldn't be wasted. We need to start now before it is too late.

Okay, I will admit that this may sound a little over the top, and that is not my intention, but that is my passion coming through. Best Friend Friday has been like my baby, and I have seen firsthand the benefits of having best friends at work and beyond. You can accomplish more together than you will ever do apart. For any company that is looking to improve their culture, I am here to say that if you don't figure this part out first, nothing you do will matter. It is people that make change happen, and if those people do not like each other and do not consider each other Best Friends, any survey or training program you roll out will fail.

If you're a leader or an employee inside the company, it doesn't matter, you have the power to start making a change by accepting the BFF challenge and playing that infinite game. You cannot stop, you must be relentless in your effort and if you do that, you will drive change and make a difference. Then when it comes time for you to play your final episode, people are going to remember the impact you had on their lives.

# CHAPTER 8

# BFF Finale

ALL GOOD THINGS must eventually come to an end. Luckily for you I am talking about this book, not Best Friend Friday. However, I would be lying if I said that I haven't thought about what the final episode of BFF would look like. I really have no exit strategy. I know in my heart that I cannot keep doing episodes every single Friday for the rest of my life, or can I? As I have said many times throughout the book, BFF is not just about the Friday videos. In reality, there will be a time when it's no longer feasible for me to do the videos. When that point will come is yet to be determined. I do ask myself from time to time, how I will end this "thing" that was originally started just to dispel the myth that we all have Best Friends at work. It was never my intention to go this long doing the videos, but I have since realized that it has become part of me, it's my "brand."

The many BFAWs in my life who have provided me words of encouragement, support, or thanks really made me start to realize that BFF is part of me and my personal brand. I think that might be the reason why I took BFF back for season 3, because I felt a passion for wanting to make people feel better at work and beyond. Your personal brand is important – it is a reflection of what you're passionate about, your values, and how you want to show up. Your brand should set you apart from others and it should demonstrate to others what you're all about. If you have a strong personal brand, it will leave a lasting impression on others and this world.

My main goal for Best Friend Friday was to use Fridays as the day we all celebrate our Best Friends in our lives, and a day we could use to meet new best friends at work or elsewhere. I want people to use Friday to be a little nicer or more patient with each other. I am not saying you should only do this one day a week – if anything I hoped you realized by reading this far that this BFF thing has nothing to do with Friday other than it was the name of the movement and a day of the week. Spending time with Best Friends and seeing what BFF has turned into should convince you that it is not just about a video of a guy in a costume every Friday asking someone else what it means to be a best friend to someone. It really was all about a stuffed bear. Kidding! They sure like that bear though.

It has been a fun ride, and I have no immediate plans of stopping at this particular moment. I continue to get ideas that randomly pop in my head, or from connecting with a BFAW and listening to their suggestions or feedback on what BFF means to them. In my heart I think it is supposed to be like this. To this day, I still don't understand why in 2019 I decided to take BFF back and share it with more of our employees outside of my department. I don't want to say it was divine intervention, but I just did.

Sometimes we do not choose the path, the path is chosen for us. Part of me is excited that I don't know what the future holds and what this BFF thing can ultimately become. I figure that if I stay true to the BFAW concepts and live the eight traits to relate, there is no stopping what BFF can turn into. Let me guess, you forgot what the eight traits were? Don't panic, I will go over them again.

I want to connect with you because you have read this book this far (or you skipped seven chapters and went to the end thinking I was going to sum the whole book up). Well, I won't sum it up entirely, but since we're Best Friends now, I will give you some key points to remember. I do want to hear your thoughts for what I should do next with BFF. I would love it if you would email me at **BFFHQ@gmail.com** to help me figure out what's next, or if you just want to connect. Sorry, this is not the place to ask for refunds on the book. By purchasing the book, you have now contributed to the stuffed bear population. Sammy Bear is in demand, and he loves meeting new BFAWs, so thank you. Now let's recap.

If you have not figured it out by now, this is all about Best Friends and meeting new people and forming relationships. I couldn't have written this book if it wasn't for the encouragement from my BFAWs and the amazing BFAWs that have been featured on BFF who shared their stories, wisdom and told us why having best friends at work was important. Honestly, I am not sure how this book is going to be received – as I said in the first chapter, who am I to write a book? Trust me, the thought that this would be an epic failure has crossed my mind, but I did it and If am forever grateful to my Best Friends who support and believe in Best Friend Friday.

Best Friend Friday is not about one guy and a bear. It's about the Best Friends that embrace the meaning of BFF and want to continue to connect with people. It's about highlighting these relationships and being there for your Best Friend. It's how you show up daily in your life and make a conscious effort to make this world better. We cannot do anything alone in this life, you need people, in one way or another, to help you along your way. We need people in our lives, and it makes it a lot better if we have long-lasting relationships with these people. What better place to find these relationships than the place where you spend most of your waking hours, the place we call work.

I wrote this book to try and explain the journey of BFF and to share some lessons I learned along the way. I have become a better person because of BFF, but honestly it was my BFAWs who made me better. The constant encouragement and thanks I have gotten over these years have been the fuel to keep it going. If you take anything away from what I have shared in the previous chapters and you commit to figure out how you will make an impact in your life, then I have succeeded in what I set out to do.

BFAW stands for Best Friend At Work. It has grown into the BFAW concepts:

**B**etter Relationships
**F**un
**A**ction
**W**hy

WHY = Action + Fun x Better Relationships

I challenge you to figure out your WHY in life. What gets you out of bed in the morning. Best Selling author Simon Sinek has written many books on this topic and there is a ton of information out there. I encourage you to look at these to get your ideas flowing. I've given you a quick way to get started by using the 3P's:

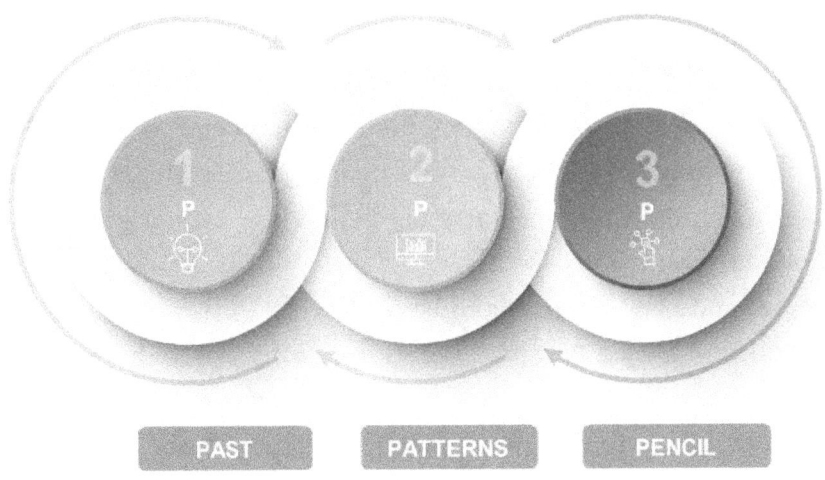

**Past** – Look at what you have done in the past. Talk with your Best Friends and ask them why they are friends with you. Getting an understanding of you as a person is the first step.

**Patterns** – As you begin to think of your past and talk with your friends, you will organically start seeing patterns in your life. What is the same about you over time?

**Pencil** – Now it is time to grab your pencil and start writing out your why. Write down all that you have explored, what your friends said about you, and draft your why. I like using a pencil instead of a pen because they are not permanent and can change easily.

Your WHY can change over time and you will never complete it in your lifetime. It is the driving force of your existence and what makes you do what you do.

Now you have to take action. That was the A in our concept. It is the driving force of getting anything accomplished and how you show up every day. We need to take the first step. I'll remind you of the teachings of Master Yoda, "do or do not there is no try." Don't be afraid to fail, "fear is the path to the dark side." Just get in there, take action, and see what happens next.

We will have Fun fun fun 'til her daddy takes the T-bird away. Yes, that Beach Boys song popped in my head when I thought about the F in our concept. Let's have fun at work! Forced Fun is the worst Fun. Fun should just come naturally by having a mindsight of how you choose to show up. We all have a little kid inside of us dying to come out and play. So, play and have some fun.

You don't need to take everything so seriously, have a playful mindsight in anything you do. We spend way too much time at work not to have fun. I know there is a time and place for everything, and you could be dealing with a serious crisis at work where it is not time to "goof around" and laugh, but honestly sometimes a little humor or calming attitude will get you through the crisis. Enjoy spending time with your Best Friends and have fun while you're working and you will see the difference, trust me – I hang out with a stuffed bear!

Finally, if you do all three of those things, you're on your way to the final element of the BFAW concept, Better Relationships. This is what it is all about, we want to have better relationships with the other humans on this planet. I practice what I like to call the eight traits to relate. These are:

Patience

Kindness

Humility

Respectfulness

Selflessness

Forgiveness

Honesty

Commitment

I encourage you all to continually push yourself to show up and practice these eight traits. I am the first to admit I am not perfect, so I understand that there might be some of the eight that you need to work on. For me, patience is a daily battle, but I am determined to get better. I really want you to engage with people and make your relationships better, and these eight can help. I am sure you're probably already practicing these, and these are not new to you, but a little reminder never hurts.

These eight traits go hand-in-hand with the philosophy introduced by my BFAW and guest star on BFF in Season 6, David Robinson. David talked about the philosophy he uses when describing best friends. David says the first thing you need to have with your best friend is TRUST. You need to have trust amongst each other at all times. The second part is Honesty, you need to have honesty between each other. You need to have someone that can tell you when to pull back or push forward. We need honesty because we all have faults. The last letter in his philosophy E stood for Empathy. You need to have the ability to understand each other and share our feelings.

David believes this is what we all should strive for in being best friends. I couldn't agree more with this philosophy, and I hope many of you already practice these. This simple philosophy is very powerful in my opinion. If you are not practicing all of these, your relationships are doomed to fail. Epic failure for sure! However, if we do this right, we will form stronger relationships at work and in our personal lives and together we can be unstoppable.

As I write the final words of the final chapter, I am literally sitting on an American Airlines flight heading home from DFW-CMH, but I am in seat 10D. If you recall from chapter one, my favorite seat is 9D. If that is not available, I move back one row. It would have been very cool to finish this up in 9D, and I guess if I write it that way you wouldn't know the difference anyway, but I am all about Honesty and Trust, trust me I am writing this in 10D. So why am

I mentioning this now? Well because I went back a row, and it has allowed me time to take a step back, reflect, and say I did it.

I took action and accomplished something I thought I could never do. A lot of this is due to encouragement from my Best Friends and the insight I gained from doing BFF. I used to be the guy that could care less about culture, and that the question about having a best friend at work was absolutely ridiculous. I have seen why having a best friend at work is so important, not only for your own wellbeing, but for an even greater purpose. If more of us practiced what I have talked about throughout this book, anything is possible. I firmly believe that having Best Friends at work is the foundation of a company's culture. Best Friend Friday (BFF) is just one day we can use to celebrate our BFAWs inside and out of work.

BFF is a framework to drive change and improve relationships at work and beyond. It is all about connecting with others and taking the action to be a best friend to someone. You will not be able to accomplish anything in your life alone, there will always be someone to help you. Life is hard enough, so it is much easier if we have best friends that we can rely on.

Take the BFF challenge and ask yourself, "What am I doing to be a best friend to someone?" Then go and do it! Start with whatever you are comfortable doing – just reach out and don't wait to start spreading the message and recognizing the BFAWs in your life. Be relentless in your action and you will see the results. If we all do this, then there is no "real" finale for BFF. It may become something that is yet to be written, but let's write the next chapter together.

I will leave you with one final thought, and if you do anything, remember this:

Best Friends can change the world!
Connect with your BFAW and help change the world!

*Me and Phil Ulrich doing the annual Thanksgiving BFF*

*Best friends make good times better and hard times better.*

Become a BFAW Today

# Acknowledgements

It must be obvious that a book about Best Friends means I have plenty of people in my life to thank. I would not be the person I am today without people being there when I needed them or even when I thought I did not. There have been so many people that have walked with me on my journey and others that were there to pick me up when I fell. I hope this book made you smile a little and you got one or two nuggets that can help you in your life. I hope you now understand that BFF may have started as a video on Friday, but every BFAW I have had on has contributed to the continued success of making people understand that we are better off if we have Best Friends at work and beyond. Also thank you to everyone who continues to follow BFF and spread the message in your circle of influence.

To my wife and best friend in life Gina, who has sacrificed so much so I could live my WHY in life. Thank you for convincing me to write this book and giving me your feedback as I completed each chapter. Yes, I know you made me who I am today.

To my sons Sammy, Vinny, and Joey. You three are my greatest achievement in life, and yes, your mother did all the heavy lifting with you all. You also sacrificed as I was not there for every moment in your life as I worked to try and give you a life you deserved. It has been my biggest regret, but together we were able to be the happy and loving family we are today. Now please give us some grandchildren so I can have new Star Wars buddies to spoil.

Thank you to my Yoda, Stan Partlow who became my best friend at work and "my person" in life. You have been so many things to me, my leader, friend, mentor, coach, father, teacher, and now book coach/editor. Thanks for editing this book and editing me in life. You have poured the water over this rock, and I will never forget the "walk around the block" that changed me forever.

Thank you, Kaitlin Brennan for being an amazing best friend, supporter, and the primary editor on this book. Your help with this has earned you one million electron points. You have been one of the kindest people I know and are always willing to help anyone that asks or even when the don't.

Thank you, Phil Ulrich for writing the foreword to this book and your continued support of Best Friend Friday. From the first time I met you, you have been an amazing champion of BFF and a friend to me. We need more people like you in this world.

Thank you, Maria Dominguez, who truly was my first Jedi Master. You saw something in me and taught me how to be a security professional. Thank you for taking me on as your padawan learner and giving me my shot when my name was not even on the list. I appreciate after 20+ years we have stayed connected, and you still provide me counsel to this day.

Thank you, Julie Sherwood, for being my mentor these last several years through some rough times in my life. You got me through some dark times and provided me the encouragement and guidance to drive through the challenges I faced. I am so grateful to have you in my circle and you have made me a better leader and friend. I owe you a lot and appreciate you more than you can ever imagine.

Thank you, Wade Smith, for being my first mentor after Stan retired and recommending Julie when you left the company. Your counsel has always been sound, and you taught me how to have an executive presence and still be my fun self.

Thank you, Christy Bertolo, for convincing me that Best Friend Friday was special and could be much more than a Friday video. You challenged me to think in a different way and was the driving force that led me to figure out the BFAW concepts. I do not know if I will ever take the leap off that cliff, but I know if I do you will be down there waiting to help me.

Thank you, David Ball for making me laugh and giving me a hard time in every meeting we are in together. You didn't let that title of yours go to your head. You are a great best friend to me and a culture champion. Please remember DATTS and know that if I am not there you can survive.

Thank you, Sean Parcel for listening anytime I needed your ear. You have been a true best friend and partner these many years and you are there for me whenever I need you. You have given me sound advice over the years and made me laugh when I needed it the most.

Thank you, Steve Swick who had the hardest job in the world. You had to manage me for part of your career. You believed in our culture and was always there for me when I needed you. Thank you for believing in me and allowing me to dip my toes into Cyber.

Thank you to my current team of employees and past employees that worked in a department I was responsible for. You have challenged me to work hard for you and made me a better leader by not accepting the status quo. We truly are family, and I cannot thank you enough for all that you do.

Finally, I want to thank all the employees and contractors at American Electric Power. Thank you BFAWs for allowing me to serve you and embracing our culture. It is the people that make our culture better. I have learned so much during my time at AEP and cannot thank you enough for supporting and embracing Best Friend Friday. You are the reason it has been so successful and know that we are changing the world, one best friend at a time.

www.ingramcontent.com/pod-product-compliance
Lightning Source LLC
Chambersburg PA
CBHW060332130626
46553CB00003B/987